SPEECH SOUNDS

Second Edition

'This is a very approachable introduction to the description and classification of the sounds of speech – not only the sounds of English, but all the various sound-types represented in the Chart of the International Phonetic Association. Dr Ashby's friendly style leads the reader through homophones and homographs, velars and alveolars, palatalization and nasalization, all with helpful practical examples and exercises. This book has rightly acquired a high reputation with teachers and learners of practical phonetics.'

John Wells, Professor of Phonetics,
University College London

Routledge Language Workbooks provide absolute beginners with practical introductions to core areas of language study. Books in the series provide comprehensive coverage of the area as well as a basis for further investigation. Each Language Workbook guides the reader through the subject using 'hands-on' language analysis, equipping them with the basic analytical skills needed to handle a wide range of data. Written in a clear and simple style, with all technical concepts fully explained, Language Workbooks can be used for independent study or as part of a taught class.

Speech Sounds:

- helps develop the fundamental skills of the phonetician
- investigates the various aspects involved in the production of speech sounds
- uses data-based material to reinforce each new concept
- includes examples from a wide range of languages
- provides dozens of exercises with solutions and cross-references
- can complement existing course or textbook material

The new edition of *Speech Sounds* has been revised and updated throughout and includes new examples and exercises, a new appendix giving information on career prospects, and a fully updated further reading section.

Patricia Ashby is Principal Lecturer in Phonetics and Coordinator for the Linguistics Evening Programme at the University of Westminster.

LANGUAGE WORKBOOKS

Series editor: Richard Hudson

Books in the series:

SPEECH SOUNDS

Second Edition

PATRICIA ASHBY

Routledge
Taylor & Francis Group

LONDON AND NEW YORK

First published 1995
by Routledge

Reprinted 1998

Second edition first published 2005
by Routledge
2 Park Square, Milton Park, Abingdon, Oxon OX14 4RN

Simultaneously published in the USA and Canada
by Routledge
270 Madison Ave, New York, NY 10016

Routledge is an imprint of the Taylor & Francis Group

© 2005 Patricia Ashby

Typeset in Galliard and Futura by
Florence Production Ltd, Stoodleigh, Devon
Printed and bound in Great Britain by
TJ International Ltd, Padstow, Cornwall

British Library Cataloguing in Publication Data
A catalogue record for this book is available from the British
Library

Library of Congress Cataloging in Publication Data
Ashby, Patricia.
  Speech sounds/Patricia Ashby – 2nd ed.
     p. cm.
   Includes index.
  1. Phonetics.   I. Title.
  P221.A78 2005
  414′.8–dc22   2004026304

ISBN 0–415–34177–9 (hbk)
ISBN 0–415–34178–7 (pbk)

CONTENTS

ILLUSTRATIONS

USING THIS BOOK

This book aims to get you started on the theory and practice of phonetics, the study of speech.

It deals with the kind of phonetics which can be done by listening analytically to speech, or by attending closely to our own activities as speakers. It is not concerned with the kind of phonetics that involves making machine measurements of speech sounds, or measurements of the activities of speakers. Whatever your ultimate concern with speech, the same basic skills and knowledge are needed, so the book deals with these basics – the way in which speech sounds are produced, and how they can be described, classified and represented.

There is a fair amount of technical terminology in this subject. This is unavoidable if we want to describe speech with any degree of precision. It is important to keep in mind that this is finite and to try not to let it put you off! In the margins of each chapter **keywords** are presented in bold print as they occur. The first use of each term is in capitals, and the accompanying text gives a full explanation and definition. Each term represents an important concept, so try to master the terminology as you go along. One possibility is to treat these as you would new vocabulary when learning a foreign language – keep a vocabulary list and learn the definition and an example of each new term as it arises.

Each chapter has **Exercises** designed to prepare you for real data analysis. Answers, often with explanations, are given at the end of the book, but be sure to try the problems for yourself before looking up the answers. Where necessary, the answers are supported in the text itself by a comment section – again, don't read this before you have had a really good go at the exercise for yourself. Each chapter has a **Summary** which brings together the main learning points of the chapter and some chapters have **Further Exercises** to consolidate your new skills.

Phonetics is not just a matter of what you can hear. What we can see when we watch a speaker and what we can sense about our own speech movements are also vital sources of information. The workbook is designed to help you develop your awareness of speech, whether you are working alone or with a group of other students and a teacher. If the text recommends looking in a mirror, then do just that.

Where you see a small speech balloon in the margin you will find an exercise that requires you to speak aloud, think consciously about the movements you are making or concentrate specifically on the sounds that result.

If the book accomplishes what it sets out to do, many of you will want to follow things up, so the book concludes with advice on **Further Reading**, with suggestions on the different directions in which your study of phonetics may now take you.

ACKNOWLEDGEMENTS

As was the case with the previous edition of this book, I would like to thank my husband, Michael Ashby, for his support and the interest that he has shown in this work.

For this second edition, my thanks are now also due to very many colleagues and students who have used the book in its first edition and who have produced, over the years, a continuous stream of useful and encouraging feedback in the form of comments, suggestions and helpful criticism. All this invaluable advice has been greatly appreciated and, where possible, implemented.

Exercise data are still of my own compilation and continue to benefit from examples (simplified or adapted here) from a number of rather older publications, which continue to be a valuable gold-mine of source materials:

Demers, R. A. and A. K. Farmer (1986) *A Linguistics Workbook*. Cambridge, MA: MIT Press.

Gleason Jr, H. A. (1955) *Workbook in Descriptive Linguistics*. New York: Holt, Rinehart & Winston.

Halle, M. and G. N. Clements (1983) *Problem Book in Phonology*. Cambridge, MA: MIT Press.

Langacker, R. W. (1972) *Fundamentals of Linguistic Analysis*. New York: Harcourt Brace Jovanovich.

Pike, K. L. (1947) *Phonemics*. Ann Arbor: University of Michigan Press.

The vowel diagram for French (Exercise 8.3) follows P. MacCarthy (1975) *The Pronunciation of French*. Oxford: Oxford University Press.

PERMISSIONS

The author and publishers gratefully acknowledge permission from the following to quote from copyright materials:

Jonathan Raban and PanMacmillan for the extract from *Coasting* by Jonathan Raban.

PanMacmillan and the Wylie Agency Inc. for the extract from *Awakenings* by Oliver Sacks, copyright © 1991 by Oliver Sacks, reprinted with the permission of the Wylie Agency Inc.

HarperCollins Publishers Ltd for the extract from *The Phantom Tollbooth* by Norton Juster, copyright © 1988 Norton Juster.

HarperCollins Publishers Ltd for the extract from *On Cats* by Doris Lessing, copyright © 2002 Doris Lessing.

HarperCollins Publishers Ltd for the extract from *Something Wholesale* by Eric Newby, copyright © 1985 Eric Newby.

Every effort has been made to trace copyright holders although this has not been possible in every case.

SPOKEN AND WRITTEN LANGUAGE

1

This chapter is concerned with the difference between spoken and written forms of language. The concepts 'speech sound', 'vowel' and 'consonant' are introduced. We also begin to explore differences between different varieties of spoken English.

SPEECH AND WRITING

Say aloud the English word *peace* in your usual pronunciation. Repeat it several times, and then compare your pronunciation of the word written *piece*. You will probably find that you pronounce the two words in exactly the same way. The words are written differently, and have different meanings, but for nearly all native speakers of English there is not the slightest difference between them in sound. Words which are pronounced identically are called HOMOPHONES (*homo-* 'same' + *phone* 'sound').

Homophone

EXERCISE

1.1 At least some of the English words in the following groups will be homophones for you. Try to decide which are and which aren't.

boy	buoy
led	lead (metal)
fool	full
weight	wait
horse	hoarse
which	witch

groan	grown		
luck	look		
maize	maze	May's	
sees	seas	seize	C's
or	awe	oar	ore

Comment

There is no single set of 'right' answers to this exercise – the answers you give will depend in part on the type of English you speak. For instance *fool* and *full* are homophones for many Scots, but not for speakers from England or Wales. Try to make objective decisions about your own speech, and then if possible collect answers from a speaker whose English sounds different from yours.

The homophones we have just considered happen to have distinct spellings, but this is not always the case. For instance, there are three different words *tick* in English:

tick (the mark ✓)
tick ('credit'. For instance: *he bought it on tick*)
tick (parasite living on cattle, etc.)

Similarly, there are three homophonous words all spelt *till*:

till (= until)
till (to dig and cultivate the ground)
till (cash register)

Homograph Words which are written the same way (regardless of how they are pronounced) are termed HOMOGRAPHS (*homo-* 'same' + *graph* 'writing'). The words *read* (rhymes with *feed*) and *read* (rhymes with *bed*) show us that English words can be spelt the same way yet pronounced differently. So not all homophones are homographs, and not all homographs are homophones. The general conclusion is that sameness and difference of sound is a completely different issue from sameness or difference of spelling.

LETTERS AND SOUNDS

The word *cat* has three letters *c*, *a* and *t*. Most people can agree that it also has three sounds. We can say the word slowly, splitting it up into parts and counting them out on our fingers. But letters and sounds are not at all the same things. The word *cough* has five letters in spelling – but when we say it, it too only has three sounds. The first is like the first sound of *kite*, the second is like the middle sound of *top*, and the last is like the end of *roof*. A more logical spelling for the word might be *kof* – and in fact young children learning to write English do invent such spellings. More reliable than makeshift spellings are PHONETIC TRAN-SCRIPTIONS using internationally agreed SYMBOLS; our own British pronunciation of the word is then [kɒf] (the square brackets are just a convention to show that the symbols are to be taken as phonetic tran-scription). One principle governing the use of phonetic symbols is that there should be one symbol for every sound; the number of letters in the ordinary spelling is simply irrelevant.

Phonetic transcription

Symbol

EXERCISE

1.2 How many sounds have each of the following English words?

1. dog	2. moon	3. fish	4. bath
5. rabbit	6. enough	7. study	8. through
9. spaghetti	10. tricky		

Comment

As you can see, there is not a simple relationship between letters and sounds in English speech at all. First, some letters are altogether 'silent'. In the example *through* above, the letters *gh* are 'silent'. The spelling *thru* records the same pronunciation. Notice also that *threw* is a homophone. (Examples of other 'silent' letters are *h* in *hour*, the second *b* in *bomb*, *p* in *psychology*.) Second, it sometimes takes several letters to 'spell' one sound. What's written *th* at the end of *bath* we hear as a single sound – as we'll see, it is represented with the single symbol [θ]. Likewise, *sh* at the end of *fish* stands for one sound [ʃ], *gh* in *enough* represents the sound [f] (but in *spaghetti*, it represents [g]). The *oo* in the middle of *moon* represents just one sound (the symbol in fact is [u]); and the *bb* and *tt* in *rabbit* and *spaghetti* represent just one sound each, [b] and [t]. If you are not sure about this last point, see if you can say *rabbit* with two *b*'s in the middle. If you can, you will recognize that it sounds a bit like a stammer, or perhaps as if you were saying a phrase some-thing like *rab a bit*. The letters *ck*, as in *tricky*, always represent just one sound, a [k].

Vowel

Consonant

The individual speech sounds that we have begun to discover fall into two groups: VOWELS and CONSONANTS. Every human speech sound is either a vowel or a consonant. When the doctor asks you to open your mouth and say 'Ah', he is asking you to make a vowel type of sound. We can represent it (for now – there's a bit more detail to come later) with the symbol [ɑ]. Something like this vowel will occur in your pronunciation of the word *farm*. The other sounds in the word are consonants; they are [f], [m] and – for some speakers – [r] (for other speakers, the *r* is silent). Look in a mirror and notice how in the vowel [ɑ] your mouth is wide open, whereas in consonants such as [f] and [m] the mouth is closed or nearly closed. Vowel sounds always have a relatively free outward flow of breath; in typical consonant sounds the flow of breath is temporarily obstructed or blocked.

In English, as in all other languages, the majority of words are composed of vowels and consonants used together – e.g. *farm, rabbit, peace, through*. It's also possible to find English words that consist only of vowel-type sounds: for instance *eye* and *owe*. (Don't be fooled by the letters *y* and *w* into thinking that these words must contain consonants; notice that *eye* is a homophone of *I*, and that *owe* is a homophone of *Oh* and *O*.) However, there are no proper English words which consist only of consonants. The nearest we come to this is a few examples of sustained consonant sounds used as exclamations: *Shh!, Brr!, Mm!*

The distinction between vowel and consonant is of crucial importance in the description of languages. Here is a simple example from English. The indefinite article has two different forms: *a* and *an*. Compare *a pear* and *an apple*. The two forms of the indefinite article are not simply variants which can be interchanged. Notice that we can't say *a apple* or *an pear*.

EXERCISE

1.3 What form of the indefinite article is required with the following nouns, and what is the rule that governs the choice between *a* and *an*?

1.	farm	2.	eye	3.	shop	4.	island
5.	mouth	6.	union	7.	onion	8.	ewe
9.	yacht	10.	one	11.	eunuch	12.	hair
13.	heir	14.	umpire	15.	hour	16.	week

Comment

The choice between *a* and *an* clearly depends on whether the following word begins with a vowel or a consonant. Before a vowel sound, *an* is required (*an apple*, *an island*); before a consonant sound, *a* is used. The decision can't be made on the basis of spelling. Notice that since we get *a union*, *a ewe* and *a eunuch*, these words must actually begin with consonant sounds (though spelt with vowel letters). In fact, they all begin with the same consonant represented as spelling letter *y* in the word *yacht*. Similarly, since we find *a one* rather than *an one*, this must indicate that the word *one* is pronounced with an initial consonant sound; in fact it's the same consonant as heard at the beginning of *week*. Finally, although the sound [h] is a consonant (*a hair*), in some words the letter *h* is silent. These words therefore begin with a vowel sound in speech: *an hour*, *an heir*. In a very few words, you can choose: *a hotel* or *an (h)otel*. (Of course, a few accents leave out h-sounds altogether – for speakers of such accents, all so-called *h*-words will begin with a vowel.)

EXERCISE

1.4 Which of the following items begin with a consonant sound?

1. honour	2. year	3. usual	4. once
5. X-ray	6. oomph	7. young	8. U-turn
9. who	10. euphonium		

CV PATTERNS

If we write the capital letter C to mean 'any consonant' and V to mean 'any vowel', we can represent the basic sound structure of a word as a string of Cs and Vs. For instance *peace* has the pattern CVC; *rabbit* is CVCVC.

EXERCISE

1.5 Represent the following words using the symbols C and V.

1. do	2. flea	3. help	4. brand
5. enough	6. dispute	7. spaghetti	8. tax
9. through	10. tacks		

For the words used in Exercise 1.5, the answers are largely unaffected by the particular type of English which you speak. But there are other words over which speakers will differ. We have seen already that *farm* is either CVC or CVCC depending on whether your type of English actually pronounces any sound corresponding to the *r* of the spelling. A similar difference affects many other words. For instance *art* is either VC or VCC, *car* is either CV or CVC. This difference in the treatment of *r* is the most fundamental feature distinguishing different types of English accent. If you pronounce an r-sound in all the places where there is *r* in the spelling, you have what is called a RHOTIC ACCENT. This is typical of General American speech and the pronunciation of English in Scotland, Ireland and the south-western part of England.

Rhotic accent

Non-rhotic accent

On the other hand, a NON-RHOTIC ACCENT has no r-sound in *farm*, *art* or *car*. In fact r-sounds are allowed when a vowel follows immediately, as it does, for instance in *red*, *bread*, *very*. Non-rhotic speech is found in most of England (apart from the South West), and in Wales, Australia, New Zealand and South Africa. The author of this book has a non-rhotic accent.

EXERCISE

1.6 Use C and V to show the structure of the following words in (a) a rhotic accent, (b) a non-rhotic accent.

1. near   2. nearer   3. farmer   4. colour
5. colouring   6. strawberry   7. mirror   8. hard
9. father   10. further   11. postcard   12. wrestler

The concepts introduced so far will all be taken up and refined in later chapters. In the next chapter we start to learn phonetic symbols and to read and write phonetic transcriptions.

SUMMARY

- Words with the same pronunciation (regardless of spelling) are called homophones.
- Accents can differ in the way in which they pronounce words.
- All words, when spoken aloud, are made up of sequences of vowel sounds and consonant sounds.
- Each sound, vowel or consonant, has its own unique symbol which we use to represent it in phonetic transcription.

FURTHER EXERCISES

1.7 Complete the table for the following English words. Some examples are given.

		Homophones?	Homographs?
boy	buoy	+	–
read (present tense)	read (past tense)	–	+
breed	bread	–	–
bank (for money)	bank (of river)	+	+
son	sun		
bill (of bird)	bill (= invoice)		
seen	scene		
eyes	ice		
tear (in the eye)	tear (= rip)		
flee	flea		
fleas	fleece		
tick	tic		

1.8 Using items from any of the exercises in this chapter, practise:

1. deciding whether they begin with a vowel sound or a consonant sound;
2. deciding whether they end with a vowel sound or a consonant sound;
3. writing CV formulas.

Discuss your answers with a friend. If you do not agree, try to decide why – is one of you right and the other wrong, or do you have different accents?

2 PHONETIC TRANSCRIPTION, CONSONANT AND VOWEL SOUNDS

In this chapter we build on what you already know about the roman alphabet and about the pronunciation of your kind of English to get you started reading and writing phonetic transcription in a variety of languages.

READING PHONETIC TRANSCRIPTIONS

Anyone who is literate in English – and since you're reading this, that must by definition include you – already knows a surprising amount about speech sounds and the symbols used to represent them. Try reading aloud the following – you already know what to do without having to be told.

1. [sed]
2. [ment]
3. [frend]
4. [nekst]
5. [ne]
6. [me]

The first four, when spoken, are clearly English words – you'll have recognized *said, meant, friend, next*. Item 5 is the Greek word meaning 'yes'; you will have pronounced it correctly provided you made it just like the beginning of 4. When you said 6, again assuming that you were being consistent and pronouncing it just like the beginning of 2, you were saying the Japanese word for 'eye'.

International Phonetic Alphabet

The INTERNATIONAL PHONETIC ALPHABET (hereafter, IPA) provides about two hundred symbols for the sounds encountered in the world's languages, but it is based upon the roman alphabet (which you already know). You are also familiar with at least one variety of English speech. True, English is just one among five thousand or so languages in the world, but it provides a reasonable sampling of human speech sounds. In fact, English has a somewhat complex sound system, and the work you did in mastering that (whether as a child acquiring your first language, or as an adult learner of English) gives you a head start in phonetics.

CONSONANT SOUNDS AND SYMBOLS

Subject to a few cautions which we'll come to shortly, the following symbols mean exactly what you'd expect:

m n b p d t g k f v s z w r l h

Here are English words which have these consonants in initial position:

[m]	mike	[f]	foxtrot
[n]	november	[v]	victor
[b]	bravo	[s]	sierra
[p]	papa	[z]	zebra
[d]	delta	[w]	wellington
[t]	tango	[r]	romeo
[g]	golf	[l]	lima
[k]	kilo	[h]	hercules

EXERCISE

2.1 Write representations for the following words, using phonetic symbols for the consonant sounds and representing each vowel simply as V.

1. cabinet	2. telephone	3. umbrella
4. September	5. ghost	6. whosoever
7. centipede	8. melancholy	9. photographic
10. beeswax	11. cellophane	12. quibble

Here are the cautions we mentioned. First, when we use them to represent sounds, we never call them 'letters', but symbols. Second, when we write them by hand we don't use our ordinary cursive handwriting, but carefully formed shapes that copy the printed forms fairly closely. Illegible phonetic symbols would clearly be useless. Third, you must remember that each symbol always and everywhere has the same sound value, with none of the variations and inconsistencies we're used to from ordinary English spelling. So [g] always has the value of the first sound in *golf*, never the first sound in *gin* (the word *gin* in fact begins with a sound for which we haven't yet given the symbol). There are no 'silent' symbols and no combinations like *ph* in *photo*; the symbols [ph] would actually mean the sound sequence which occurs in the middle of *peephole* (provided, in your accent, you pronounce the h-sound). Finally, a word of warning about the [r] symbol: at the moment, we are just using this shape to mean any kind of r-sound. Later, we will learn some rather more specialized symbols for different kinds of r-sound.

MORE VOWELS

We are almost ready to attempt reading and writing more examples of phonetic transcription, but at the moment we are a bit short of vowels. The only vowel symbol we've used so far (apart from a brief mention of [ɒ] in cough [kɒf], [u] in *moon* and [ɑ] in *Ah!* on pp. 3 and 4) is [e] as in *next* [nekst], *red* [red], etc. But letter *e* in English spelling doesn't always represent this sound. When you looked at the Japanese word [me] (eye), which was example (6) above, you had to resist the temptation to say the English word *me*, which in fact is pronounced [mi]. From this you gather that [i] has the value familiar to you in words like *ski, kiwi*. We are now in a position, then, to write a phonetic representation for the words *peace* and *piece*; they are both pronounced [pis]. Clearly, if words are homophones, they will be identical when put into transcription.

Another vowel we can practise at this stage is [u], which means a sound of the general type you will have in *Zulu* or the first syllable of *rhubarb*. So for most speakers (the pronunciation may be different if you are Welsh, for example) *blue* is [blu], *do* is [du] and *Zulu* is actually [zulu].

We'll also add [ɑ]. This stands for a vowel of the type you will probably have in *palm* or *Zhivago*. Such a vowel is made with quite a wide, open mouth. Not all speakers will have exactly the same quality of [ɑ]-type vowel, of course, but for the moment we will just use the one symbol [ɑ]. The important thing at this stage is that you use a vowel that is made with your mouth as wide open as possible. Of course, not every *a* in spelling represents this vowel. In the word *Java*, for example, the first vowel sound is [ɑ] for a great many speakers, but the second vowel is never a repeat of the first one. To see this, try saying the word *Java* deliberately making the second vowel the same as the first – the result isn't like anyone's normal pronunciation of the word. Another example of this vowel type occurs in the first syllable of *father* for many speakers. Moreover, if you're a non-rhotic speaker you should find that the second vowel of *father* is in fact the same as the second vowel of *Java*.

EXERCISE

2.2 Now try reading these transcribed words of Dyirbal (an Australian language from North Queensland).

[pigin]	'shield'
[pɑbil]	'slice, peel'
[tɑndu]	'tree'
[tibɑn]	'stone'
[kɑgɑlum]	'moon'
[kɑbɑl]	'sand'
[pɑgɑl]	'pierce, dig'
[tudɑl]	'mash with stone'
[pugɑ]	'putrid smell'
[pulgu]	'wife'

Comment

To read these correctly, all you have to do is remember that each symbol has a consistent sound value, and try not to be put off by familiar English words and spellings. Make sure, for instance, when you read [pigin], the word for 'shield', that you are remembering to give the symbol [g] the value of the first sound in *golf*; the word should not sound like the English word *pigeon*. Notice also that the vowels are not like those in *pigeon*. Both should be [i], just as they are in English *kiwi*. When you read [pɑbil], make sure you're making the beginning like *pa*, not like *pay*, and the second part should be like the name *Beale*, not like *bill*. In all the words where [u] occurs, be careful not to insert the consonant which often accompanies the [u] type of vowel in English. The [du] at the end of [tɑndu] 'tree' should be like *do*, not like SOUTHERN BRITISH ENGLISH (SBE) *due*. SBE is the type of pronunciation generally taken as a model for foreign learners or as the codified basis for comparison with other varieties (it's the kind generally heard in international broadcasts from the BBC). Try to think how *hard* sounds when compared with *had* in that kind of accent, or how *hoard* compares with *hod*. Remember that it is a non-rhotic accent, so that *hard* and *hoard* are

Southern British English

simply CVC words. Finally here, it's worth pointing out that the [ɑ]-type vowel in SBE *hard* is pretty much the sort of vowel that is represented by the symbol [ɑ] that we introduced above.

EXERCISE

2.3 Now see if you can write some phonetic transcription yourself. Use the symbols we have learned so far to represent the pronunciations of the following English words:

1. glue
2. calm
3. cool
4. seafood
5. car-park
6. 'flu
7. rhubarb
8. ooze
9. sweet dreams
10. please

We've already pointed out that if two words are homophones, they'll be transcribed the same way, even though they are spelt differently. So [pis] corresponds to both spellings *peace* and *piece*. In the next exercise, you're asked to supply the spelling forms for the spoken forms shown. There are homophones for each one, so you need two spelling forms in each case. The symbol [r] here means an r-sound that would be pronounced in rhotic accents only (e.g. General American).

EXERCISE

2.4 Give the spelling forms for the following English words:

1. [ki]
2. [tu]
3. [buz]
4. [kruz]
5. [stil]
6. [sim]
7. [wik]
8. [blu]
9. [friz]
10. [hɑ(r)t]

So far in this chapter we've concentrated on sounds and symbols which are very much what a person who speaks and writes English would expect.

Now we add two new consonant sounds and symbols which are not so obvious.

The sound which occurs immediately before the [k] in the English word *bank* is [ŋ], called the VELAR NASAL. If you can't see at first that *bank* doesn't contain [n], try saying the word *ban* and add [k] as an afterthought. Other words with the velar nasal before [k] are *sink*, *thank*, *monkey*, *conquer*, *jinx* and many more. You will also have the velar nasal in *finger*, *longer*, *strongest*. In these, what follows is not [k], but – for most of us – [g] (some speakers will find they have no other consonant sound after the [ŋ] but go on directly to the next vowel).

Velar nasal

In some kinds of English, the velar nasal has always got to be followed by either [k] or [g]. If this is the case, then *singer* will have [ŋg] just like *finger*. This type of pronunciation is typical of some Midlands and north-western accents in England. For most of us, though, there is no [g] in *singer*, and a word like *spring* ends in a velar nasal without any following [g].

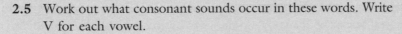

EXERCISE

2.5 Work out what consonant sounds occur in these words. Write V for each vowel.

1.	sink	2.	fang
3.	kingdom	4.	beginning
5.	banger	6.	plonk
7.	increasing	8.	uncoordinated
9.	unknown	10.	angry
11.	England	12.	lynx

We've given examples of [ŋ] at the ends of English words (*spring*), and within words when other sounds follow (*finger*, *monkey*). What we don't find in English is any words which begin with [ŋ]. English isn't alone in this, as there are plenty of other languages which have a velar nasal sound that can't appear at the beginnings of words (for instance Spanish, Japanese); on the other hand, we can find languages which don't have this restriction. Examples are Maori (from New Zealand), Malay and Dyirbal. While trying to find English examples, you may have thought of the name *Ngaio* (most people have heard of the New Zealand writer Ngaio Marsh, even if they haven't read any of her whodunnits). This is actually pronounced with [n] in English, but is a spelling of a Maori word pronounced with initial [ŋ]. The Malay word [ŋaŋa] means 'open' or 'gaping', as applied to the mouth. And the Dyirbal language, from which we read some examples above, has many words with initial velar nasal. For instance [ŋambal] means 'hear, listen to', and [ŋulga] means 'tomorrow'. You should practise making [ŋ] at the beginning of words, even though it will feel unfamiliar at first. One way to do this is to say a word like *thing* silently to yourself, freeze your mouth in the position for the final sound, and then go on aloud – for instance with Malay [ŋaŋa].

YOD

It comes as a surprise to most learners of phonetics that the phonetic symbol for the first sound of *yacht* is not [y], but [j]. From English spelling we're used to letter *j* representing the entirely different sound which is heard at the beginning of *jazz*. But this is one place where the IPA goes against English expectations. The initial consonant sound of *yacht, yellow, yard* is represented by the symbol [j]. So be careful not to transcribe with *y* if the sound you mean is [j], and not to read [j] as if it represented the first sound of *jazz*. The sound [j] can be conveniently referred to by the Hebrew name, *yod*.

In the spelling systems of certain other languages, the letter *j* does stand for sound [j]. An example is German. The German word spelled *ja* 'yes' begins with a yod; and the German word for 'yacht' is spelt *Jacht*. So to a person familiar with German spelling, the use of [j] as a phonetic symbol for yod seems perfectly natural.

In case you are wondering, the letter *y* does have a use as a phonetic symbol, but it represents a sound not used in English: a vowel sound of the type heard in French *lune* (moon). Obviously, people familiar only with English spelling don't automatically expect this, and nor do the French for that matter, as the vowel sound [y] is regularly spelt with *u* in French. But in the spelling system of Finnish, which also uses this vowel, [y] is spelt with *y* (and, incidentally, yod [j] is written with *j*). (The nearest English can come to the [y] sound is in the [ju]-sequence in words like *cue or pew*.)

YOD AFTER CONSONANTS

Words like *yak, yes, yogurt* which are spelled with *y* are not the only ones to have yod in English. Some words begin with yod even though there's no *y* in the spelling. For instance *ewe* is [ju] and *unique* is [junik]. Yod also occurs within words, after consonants. Most people will find they have a yod just after the [b] in *beauty*, without the yod the word would be a homophone of *booty*. In the same way *cute* has a yod which is missing in *coot.* We can transcribe the two words [kjut] and [kut] respectively. One well-known difference between most North American speech and British speech is the treatment of words like *new* or *tune.* The usual North American pronunciations have no yod; they are [nu] and [tun], the British pronunciations are [nju] and [tjun] (or a further development from [tjun] that makes it start like *chew*). Within Britain, however, speakers with East Anglian accents also say [nu] and [tun], and even go further than American speakers, dropping the yods in *beauty* and other words where they're kept by Americans. If you live in Britain, you may remember seeing produce described as *bootiful* in an advertisement; the spelling is meant to represent the word *beautiful* as spoken by an East Anglian farmer.

There are also words where speakers of one and the same variety of English differ over whether there should be a yod. For instance, do you pronounce *suit* as [sut], or [sjut]? And is *lewd* [lud] or [ljud]?

EXERCISE

2.6 Transcribe the following words as fully as you can. Where you don't yet know the appropriate phonetic symbol, write V for any vowel, C for any consonant.

  1. fumes   2. human
  3. communicate   4. lunar
  5. module   6. music
  7. computer   8. impunity
  9. speculate   10. spectacular

SUMMARY

- The IPA is a set of internationally agreed symbols for representing speech sounds; such representations are called phonetic transcriptions.
- Knowledge of the sound-values of the symbols enables you to read aloud phonetic transcriptions of languages you don't even know.
- Some symbols have well-established names like the velar nasal and yod.

FURTHER EXERCISES

Now more practice reading English from transcription. This time you will have to work a bit harder to avoid being put off by what look like familiar spelling patterns of English words.

2.7 The words given below all look like spelling forms of ordinary English words. In fact, they are to be read as items in phonetic transcription. When this is done, a different English word results in each case. Say what each word is. (A non-rhotic pronunciation is represented.)

1.	[grin]	2.	[pɑt]
3.	[hit]	4.	[nil]
5.	[plum]	6.	[bin]
7.	[slip]	8.	[tens]
9.	[rum]	10.	[tɑt]

2.8 Read aloud the following which are given in transcription. When you've worked out what they say, write them down in ordinary spelling, and then later try to put them back into transcription without looking at this exercise.

1. [iv its red mit]
2. [ken nidz ten sents]
3. [su livz nekst wik]
4. [stivz ruf liks]
5. [nilz gests sun left]
6. [pɑm triz . . . hit . . . dip blu si . . . tu wiks sun went]
7. [luz suts dɑk blu]
8. [nju brumz swip klin]
9. [bred nidz jist]
10. [menju
    pi sup
    bif stju
    red binz
    stimd liks
    stjud prunz
    krim
    ti]

Comment

Note that when a piece of transcription extends over more than one line (as in 10 above), we put one bracket at the beginning and one at the end. You do not need separate brackets round each line or round each item.

2.9 On p. 9 we gave words which exemplify the consonants [m n b p d t g k f v s z w r l h] in initial position. We chose internationally known words (most of them from the international communications code as used by pilots and air traffic controllers) in which the spelling-to-sound correspondences are obvious. Now find your own set of sixteen words, showing the same set of consonants (at any position in the word), but differently represented in spelling. For instance, instead of straightforward *mike* for [m], you might choose *co*mb or *hy*mn. What is the 'worst' spelling you can find for each sound?

The international code name for h is *hotel*, and the one for w is *whisky*. Can you figure out why we felt we couldn't use these words in our original list?

3 CONSONANTS: THE ROLE OF THE LARYNX

In this chapter we introduce the distinction between voiced and voiceless, the glottal stop and phonetic symbols for all the remaining consonants of English.

VOICE

Consider the words *seal* and *zeal*. While they are not homophones, they are clearly very similar in sound. In fact each is a word of structure CVC and the only difference between the words is in the first C. When a listener detects the difference between *seal* and *zeal*, it can only be done by distinguishing the sound [s] from the sound [z]. Make a good long [sss] (as if hissing the villain in a pantomime) and a long vigorous [zzz] (as if imitating the sound of a bee). The two sounds are very similar and in fact differ in only a single property. The sound [z] is a VOICED sound, whereas [s] is VOICELESS. A voiced sound such as [z] is accompanied by a buzz or tone which can be varied in a musical fashion to produce different pitches. A voiceless sound such as [s] has no musical pitch and can't be used to sing a tune.

Voiced
Voiceless

As air passes from the LUNGS on its way out of the body it must travel through the LARYNX (see Fig. 5.1 on p. 35), visible as the 'Adam's apple' in the neck. Within the larynx are the two VOCAL FOLDS (often, but less accurately, termed vocal 'cords'). The vocal folds operate rather like a valve that can be opened or shut. For normal quiet breathing, of course, the vocal folds must be wide apart, so that air can pass in and out. But if the folds are held gently near together, it is possible to push air through them in such a way as to cause vibration. The vibration takes the form of rapidly succeeding little openings and closings at the edges of the folds. Air that passes through is thus chopped into a series of 'puffs' or pulses, and an audible sound results.

Lungs
Larynx
Vocal folds

So voice is produced by rapid vibration of the vocal folds when they are adjusted in the right way and air is pushed between them. If you hold the 'Adam's apple' between thumb and forefinger while producing a long, loud [z] you may actually feel the vibration with your fingertips. Alternatively, block your ears with your fingers and contrast [s] and [z]. The buzz of voicing which accompanies [z] but not [s] is greatly magnified.

All vowels are voiced (try some and see) but many consonants come in voiced–voiceless pairs. Here are some other examples from English. Voiced [v] as in *vine* has a voiceless counterpart [f] as in *fine*. The word *shoe* begins with a voiceless sound, symbolized [ʃ]; its voiced counterpart, [ʒ], is heard in the middle of the word *measure*. You should produce and compare the sounds [s]–[z], [f]–[v], [ʃ]–[ʒ] to become aware of the voicing difference.

EXERCISE

3.1 Decide whether the consonant which occurs between the two vowels in these words is voiceless or voiced. Remember to think about sounds, not spellings.

1. yellow	2. easy	3. essay	4. ladder
5. leisure	6. funny	7. happy	8. brother
9. music	10. sugar	11. present	12. trophy

A consonant which is located between two vowels is called INTERVOCALIC.

Intervocalic

THE GLOTTAL STOP [ʔ]

If the vocal folds are pressed together so as to stop the flow of air altogether (as when holding one's breath) the result is called a GLOTTAL STOP. What we hear is actually a brief interval of silence, with a characteristic abrupt termination of the preceding speech sound and a similarly abrupt onset of whatever sound follows (sometimes called HARD ATTACK). A glottal stop (instead of a sound [t]) is heard in typical London pronunciations of words such as *letter*, *bottle*, *getting*. Many people (including some of those who use them) would regard such pronunciations as 'incorrect', although glottal stops are in fact widely used in many other words and phrases without being noticed. For instance in *It was getting dark*, the [t] of *it* is very likely to be replaced by a glottal stop, even by those speakers who would frown on a glottal stop in *getting*. The variability of glottal stops, and the

Glottal stop

Hard attack

fact that many of them seem to us to have something to do with [t] are just peculiarities of English. In many languages of the world glottal stops are regular consonants just like any other. Because the vocal folds are pressed together in producing a glottal stop, they cannot also be vibrating. Therefore glottal stops are not voiced.

VOICING IN PLOSIVES

Plosive

The glottal stop could more properly be termed the glottal PLOSIVE. English has six other plosives [b d g p t k]. Like the glottal stop, they also have a momentary interruption of airflow, but the blockage is made in the mouth rather than in the larynx. For example, in [b] and [p] the airflow is stopped by closing the lips. Because plosives involve a rather rapid sequence of events, you may have difficulty deciding whether they are voiced or voiceless (testing by holding your larynx or blocking your ears may not work). In fact [p t k] are voiceless and [b d g] are the corresponding voiced sounds.

GENERALIZING THE VOICED/VOICELESS DIFFERENCE

Once we have mastered the voicing difference, we can make voiceless versions of sounds which are familiar to us only in their voiced versions. For instance [m] is voiced, but we can learn to make a voiceless version of it (even though this is never used in regular adult English speech). If there is no separate symbol for a voiceless sound, we simply put the mark [̥] below the symbol for the voiced sound. An extra mark added to a letter-like symbol is called a DIACRITIC. So the voiceless counterpart of [m] is to be written [m̥]. We never add this diacritic to a symbol which already stands for a voiceless sound.

Diacritic

REMAINING ENGLISH CONSONANT SYMBOLS

There are just four more consonants in English for which we need symbols.

In most kinds of English, the word *thin* begins with a voiceless sound in which breath escapes noisily between the tip of the tongue and the upper teeth, making a voiceless dental FRICATIVE, [θ], and the word *then* begins with the corresponding voiced sound [ð]. Some other types of English don't use these sounds. In the local speech of London, *thin* and *fin* may be homophones, and *mother* may have [v] in the middle rather than [ð].

Fricative

The initial sounds of *chocolate* and *jazz* are voiceless and voiced respectively and belong to the class of sounds called AFFRICATES. Affricates can be clearly heard to have two elements in quick succession, so the symbol [dʒ], for instance, really does mean a sequence of something very like [d] followed by something like a rather brief [ʒ]. Compare *leisure*, which has [ʒ], with *ledger*, which has [dʒ]. The question of whether affricates are really one sound or two needn't bother us at the moment (actually both answers are right). For the time being we'll call them single C elements, so *jazz* is CVC, *chocolate* is CVCCVC (or possibly CVCVCVC if you pronounce a V corresponding to the second -*o*- of the spelling).

Affricate

Of the symbols introduced so far, the following stand for voiceless consonants: [p t k f θ s ʃ tʃ h ʔ]. The following symbols represent voiced consonants: [b d g v ð z ʒ dʒ m n ŋ w r l j]. Remember that vowels (we've used [i e ɑ u ɒ y] so far) are all voiced.

EXERCISES

3.2 Make a list of English words which shows every voiceless consonant in intervocalic position, and another list to show every voiced consonant in intervocalic position.

3.3 Decide whether the consonant at the beginning of the following words is voiced or voiceless.

1. catch	2. cello	3. bodge	4. name
5. photo	6. theme	7. scissors	8. judgement
9. useful	10. when	11. Xerox	12. Zeppelin
13. knock	14. rhythm	15. pneumonia	16. ghetto

3.4 Decide whether the sound at the end of the following words is voiced or voiceless.

1. as	2. cough	3. off	4. of
5. youth	6. some	7. church	8. once
9. roll	10. apartheid	11. booth	12. risked
13. blah	14. tax	15. through	16. tomb

3.5 Although English spelling makes use of both letters *s* and *z*, the distinction between voiceless sound [s] and voiced [z] is not always shown. Pronounce the following forms, and decide for each one whether it contains the voiceless sound [s] or the voiced sound [z]. Write the appropriate phonetic symbol.

1. zoo   2. ooze   3. was   4. husband
5. easy   6. blazer   7. laser   8. isn't
9. ceiling 10. rice   11. rise   12. ritz
13. use (verb, as in *Can I use your phone?*)
14. use (noun, as in *What's the use?*)
15. advise (verb, as in *Who can advise me?*)

3.6

(a) When nouns are made plural in English, the ending which is added is not always pronounced the same way; compare *cats*, which has [s], with *dogs*, which has [z]. Read the English nouns transcribed below (check any vowels you don't know with the discussion on pp. 10 and 11) and then copy out the transcription adding the appropriate plural ending.

1. [net]   2. [ʃak]   3. [rif]   4. [stɑ]
5. [sliv]   6. [tri]   7. [kjub]   8. [leg]
9. [lip]   10. [ʃu]   11. [tʃam]   12. [sin]

(b) Find another twenty nouns (for the time being, avoid any which end in the sounds [s], [z], [ʃ], [ʒ], [tʃ] or [dʒ]). Transcribe at least the consonants they contain, and work out how they would form their plurals. Can you see any pattern in the selection of [s] or [z] as the plural ending?

THE *WH*-SOUND AND SYMBOL

Note that if you are a speaker with a Scottish English accent, for example, you may also wish to introduce one further symbol which will enable you to note the difference between the sound you make at the beginning of *wear* (a [w]-sound) and the one you make at the beginning of *where*. In the case of words beginning *wh*- you will probably find that you make a voiceless sound which some people describe as 'pronouncing the *h*' here. The full name for the sound is a voiceless labial–velar fricative and the symbol you need is [ʍ].

THE SYMBOL FOR ENGLISH 'R'

So far, we have written the symbol for the English r-sound the right way up, like a normal printed or orthographic letter *r*. This is OK as long as we are only dealing with one language and that language only has one r-sound. However, the real phonetic symbol for English 'r' is much less convenient: it is the same shape, but written upside down [ɹ]! For the time being, at least, we don't need to worry about this, but later on we will be talking in more detail about precise phonetic values and about r-sounds in other languages and then we will have to be more pernickety about symbols.

SUMMARY

- Voice in speech is produced by vibratory activity of the vocal folds in the larynx affecting the EGRESSIVE PULMONIC AIRSTREAM.
- Sounds accompanied by this vibratory activity are said to be voiced, sounds without it are voiceless.
- All vowels are voiced but consonants vary – some are voiced, some voiceless.
- If the vocal folds are pressed firmly together and prevent the escape of lung air, a voiceless sound called a glottal stop is produced.

Egressive pulmonic airstream

FURTHER EXERCISES

3.7 Every English word contains at least one voiced segment (why?) but not every word contains a voiceless segment. In fact, whole phrases and sentences can be concocted that do not contain any voiceless segments (e.g. *I'm worried by Lilian's wandering around Venezuela alone*). What is the longest all-voiced sequence you can devise?

3.8 Turn back to the words from Dyirbal given in Exercise 2.2.

   1. Make a list of all the voiceless consonants in the words.
   2. Make a list of all the voiced consonants.
   3. Make a list of all the plosives.
   4. What observations can you make about the positions within words where voiceless consonants seem to occur in Dyirbal?

3.9 What aspect of English pronunciation is being focused on when a newspaper writes *yoof culture* (for *youth culture*)? Use phonetic symbols to show the two pronunciations, and describe the consonants involved as fully as you can.

3.10 In a *Sunday Times* article on changing standards in pronunciation, a cartoon showed *Gatwick* as *Ga wick*, and *football* as *foo ball*. What pronunciations are intended, and why do you think a gap was used to suggest them?

3.11 Some practical exercises on speech and breathing.

1. The basis of all normal speech is a controlled outflow of breath from the lungs. To see this, sustain a vowel such as [ɑ] for as long as possible, or count aloud for as long as you can. Sooner or later you have to stop to breathe in.
2. It is possible to reverse the normal state of affairs and speak on air which is being drawn into the lungs. Most people can do this at once when the possibility is suggested; children often do it for fun. It tends to produce a strange-sounding type of voice, varying out of control between a squeaky high pitch and a very low creaky pitch. Try *Good morning* like this or try to read aloud a few lines from a newspaper. From time to time you'll have to pause – but this time you'll be breathing *out* when you pause.

MORE ABOUT VOWELS

4

In this chapter we will introduce more vowel symbols, including all those needed to represent most varieties of English. We will also show how vowel sounds can be classified and described.

VOWEL QUALITY AND DURATION

In general terms, vowels are voiced sounds in which the mouth is relatively open, allowing air to flow out freely. Sometimes the mouth is wide open, as in [ɑ], sometimes less open as in [e] or [i]. The lips, too, have a part to play: in the [u] of [mun] (*moon*) the lips make a rounded opening to the mouth. If you consciously prevent them from doing this, the [u] simply won't come out right (try it and see). So different positions of the tongue, jaw and lips give recognizably different vowel sounds (different VOWEL QUALITIES).

In addition to this, languages quite often make use of LENGTH (DURATION) differences, so that some vowels (in the language in question) can be described as 'short' or '(somewhat) shorter' and others as 'long' or '(somewhat) longer'. In many kinds of English, the word *bin* has a shorter vowel, while *bean* has a longer one. Up to this point, we've been representing the vowel of *bean* with the symbol [i], but if you have looked into a dictionary that gives pronunciations you will have seen transcriptions like [biːn]. The mark [ː] (like a colon, but formed from two triangles rather than round dots – although in the handwritten form, for speed, we usually just write two dots) is there to show that the preceding sound is long in duration. In the usual transcription of British English, the length mark accompanies five of the vowel symbols: [iː] as in *heed*, [ɑː] as in *hard* (so far we've written just [ɑ]), [uː] as in *food* (so far – except in the answers to Exercise 3.4, where we compared Scottish and

Southern English pronunciations of the word *booth* – we've written just [u]), [ɔː] as in *hoard*, [ɜː] as in *heard/herd*. That's because on the whole, these vowels are pronounced longer in SBE than vowels such as those in *bin, bed*, etc. Don't mistake the extra length of *hard* and *hoard* for an r-sound that isn't there! Not all accents of English make use of vowel length in this way. You should try and decide whether length differences are important in your own accent. If they aren't, it simply means that the length mark [ː] isn't needed in transcriptions of your own type of speech.

SOUTHERN BRITISH ENGLISH VOWELS

Below is a list of words, transcribed in the type of British accent we have just mentioned, showing all the different vowel qualities which are used in that kind of speech. Read the words aloud, noting any places where you think your own speech may be different from the kind we've symbolized. Then find two more words to illustrate each vowel.

[iː]	*heed*	[hiːd]	
[ɪ]	*hid*	[hɪd]	
[e]	*head*	[hed]	
[æ]	*had*	[hæd]	
[ʌ]	*Hudd*	[hʌd]	also in *cup, love*, etc.
[ɜː]	*heard*	[hɜːd]	*herd* is a homophone
[ɑː]	*hard*	[hɑːd]	
[ɒ]	*hod*	[hɒd]	
[ɔː]	*hoard*	[hɔːd]	*horde* is a homophone
[ʊ]	*hood*	[hʊd]	
[uː]	*who'd*	[huːd]	or *food, moon*, etc.

We will return later to ways in which your own speech may be different from this. For the time being, enough of your vowels will be sufficiently similar for us to get on to the next stage in the description.

Say over the vowels symbolized [iː], [ɪ], [e], [æ]; whatever may be the precise values of these vowels as you pronounce them, it should be clear to you that your tongue starts in a fairly high position for [iː] and moves lower for each of the others (your jaw will probably be opening too, to help the tongue move down). We say that [iː] is a HIGH vowel, while [æ] is fairly LOW. (You may find that you could go a bit lower still than the usual position for [æ]; the vowel you get to can be symbolized [a].) The terms CLOSE and OPEN are equivalent to high and low respectively.

High/Close

Low/Open

EXERCISE

4.1 In each of the following pairs of words, show which word has the **closer** (= higher) vowel.

1. hot food	2. red book
3. green grass	4. six men
5. four feet	6. first scheme
7. her arm	8. see red
9. felt hat	10. damp mist

Compare your vowels [e] and [ɒ] (say a phrase like *red hot*, for example, or *set off* and then try to say the vowels on their own); it may help if you silently alternate the two mouth positions. You should become aware that in [e] you are using a part of your tongue that is well forward in your mouth; for [ɒ], however, the part of the tongue being used is much further back within the mouth. Here, then, is a second dimension for the description of tongue position in vowels. You'll find that [i] and [ɪ] also use the front part of the tongue, while [uː] and [ɑː] use the back part like [ɒ]. So vowels can be FRONT or BACK, independently of whether **Front** they are high or low. The two dimensions (front–back, high–low) map **Back** out a space which represents all the possible tongue positions in vowels. (A diagram of the tongue can be found in Fig. 5.3 on p. 36 – the labels 'front', 'centre' and 'back' show which part of the tongue is active in producing the 'front', 'central' and 'back' vowels respectively in the vowel diagram below. A surprisingly small part of the tongue is used in making vowel sounds.)

THE VOWEL DIAGRAM

The space is drawn as a four-sided figure (a quadrilateral – see Fig. 4.1) with a sloping front (because open front vowels have the active part of the tongue a bit further back than close ones and because this makes the line longer which reflects the wider gap between the two jaws at the front of the mouth when the mouth is wide open). The shape was originally derived from X-ray pictures of vowel production, but has been simplified to make it easy to draw. Vowels between high and low can be termed MID; vowels between front and back are called CENTRAL. Be **Mid** careful to distinguish these two terms; notice, for instance, that the vowel **Central** of the word *red* is a mid vowel, but not a central vowel.

4.1

A vowel diagram
with approximate
values for SBE
simple vowels

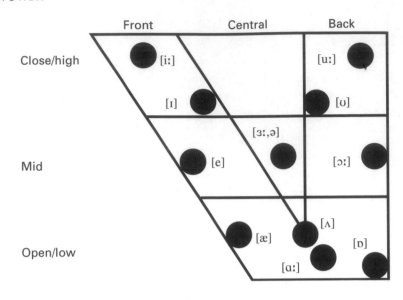

We have already decided that lip position is an important factor in vowel description. Some rounding of the lips is usual in the English vowels we are writing [ɒ], [ɔː], [ʊ] and [uː], whereas all the others are said with unrounded lips. We now have everything we need to give fairly complete descriptions of vowels; for instance, we can say that [e] is a mid front UNROUNDED vowel, and that [uː] is HIGH (or close) back ROUNDED. Of course, the lip position is quite separate from the tongue position. If we like, we can take away the lip rounding from those vowels which usually have it, leaving their tongue positions unchanged. You'll find that speakers vary in how much rounding they use for 'rounded' vowels in English. In casual speech, [uː] may have very little lip rounding for some people.

Unrounded
Rounded

EXERCISES

4.2 Read and identify the following words, and indicate whether the vowel they contain (in the pronunciation shown) is **rounded** or **unrounded**.

1. [muːn]
2. [kɔːt]
3. [hiːp]
4. [glaːs]
5. [kʊd]
6. [krʌm]
7. [ʃʌv]
8. ['piːpl]
9. [wɜːd]
10. [haːt]

(The mark ['] is a STRESS MARK, placed just before the syllable within the word which carries the greatest force or emphasis.)

Stress mark

4.3 Compare the lip positions in the two vowels of the following phrases. Are they **rounded** or **unrounded**?

1.	keep cool	2.	drop dead
3.	hang on	4.	cool off
5.	look up	6.	see through
7.	fall in	8.	work loose
9.	push back	10.	get lost

In the same way, because lip rounding is a separate thing from tongue position, we can also add lip rounding to tongue positions which hitherto we've only used for unrounded vowels. For example, if you take the tongue position for [iː] and add lip rounding to it, you obtain a close front rounded vowel, very similar to what is required in the French word *lune* (moon); the symbol for this is [y], so the French word can be transcribed [lyn].

SCHWA

There is another so-called short vowel which we did not include in the list above, because it never comes in the stressed syllables of words in this accent. But it is very important and requires a separate discussion. We pointed out earlier that the two vowels of *Java* are not identical. The first is [ɑː], a relatively long open unrounded vowel between central and back. The second is a rather short unrounded mid central vowel which we write with a turned letter *e* as [ə]; so the word is ['dʒɑːvə]. The name for the second vowel is SCHWA. Of all English vowels, schwa is the one used most often: in running speech, about one vowel in every four will be a schwa – even though English spelling has no consistent way of writing it. If we consider only the words used in this paragraph, we find it in *the*, *above*, *never*, *syllables*, *of*, *earlier*, *that*, *relatively*, *about*, *a*, *consider*, *paragraph*. To hear the schwa in *the*, *of*, *that*, *a*, be sure you are pronouncing the words as you would in running speech. If you pronounce those words on their own out of context you may find you alter the vowels. (What vowels do you change them to?)

Schwa

EXERCISE

4.4 Indicate all the examples of schwa in the following text – remember to try and pronounce it as you would in running speech.

> At the gate of the town the conqueror paused and stopped to drink from a bottle of wine that a soldier produced from a bag. At a sign from the Emperor the troops advanced and entered the town. Applause greeted them for the conqueror was popular. The tyrant ruler of former days was brought to the executioner from the prison cells. But the conqueror was generous and spared the man's life – a gesture that led to murmurs of disapproval from the assembled crowd as they remembered the tortures they had suffered.

The vowel [ɜː] of *heard* or *herd* is also an unrounded mid central vowel. This can be thought of as a sort of long schwa. Both schwas occur together in *murmur* [ˈmɜːmə] or *occur* [əˈkɜː]. In some rhotic accents (such as those of North America) the vowel corresponding to [ɜː] sounds as if an [r] has been spread right through the vowel, and we speak of an r-coloured vowel. You should practise imitating this, and see if you can **R-colouring** add R-COLOURING to other vowel types, too.

EXERCISE

4.5 In the passage in Exercise 4.4 above, which word would have the long version of schwa, [ɜː], in SBE? Would your accent have this? Would it have the [ɜː]-vowel (or something close to it) anywhere else in this passage?

Pure vowel/
Simple vowel/
Monophthong

Diphthong/
Gliding vowel/
Complex vowel

All the vowels we have discussed so far seem to have a single, fairly steady quality; they are said to be PURE VOWELS, SIMPLE VOWELS or MONO-PHTHONGS. But there's another type, DIPHTHONGS (sometimes called GLIDING VOWELS or COMPLEX VOWELS), which have a quality that is rapidly changing as time goes by. The vowel of *voice* is like this. We write it [ɔɪ] because it sweeps from something like the quality we represent [ɔ] towards something like the quality we represent [ɪ]. Another diphthong is heard in *high*: the starting point is with the mouth quite wide open, a quality we write [a], while the finishing point is quite similar to the one of the diphthong already described in *voice*. The word *house*, on the other hand, gives us a diphthong that starts rather like that of *high* but moves in a different direction; we write it [aʊ]. There are eight diphthongs in the kind of English we are describing:

[aɪ]	*buy*	[baɪ]	
[aʊ]	*bow*	[baʊ]	rhymes with *how*; *bough* is a homophone
[əʊ]	*bow*	[bəʊ]	rhymes with *go*; *beau* is a homophone
[eɪ]	*bay*	[beɪ]	
[ɔɪ]	*boy*	[bɔɪ]	
[ɪə]	*beer*	[bɪə]	
[eə]	*bear*	[beə]	*bare* is a homophone
[ʊə]	*boor*	[bʊə]	'clumsy, ill mannered person' – as in *boorish*

We have chosen *boor* as an example for the sake of comparison with the other diphthongs, but it is difficult to give a reliable keyword, since most words with [ʊə] can alternatively be pronounced with [ɔː] in this accent. Some other words where [ʊə] is fairly likely are *cure, jury, mature*. Some common words where [ɔː] is most likely to be found instead are *poor, sure, moor* and *tour*.

We can show diphthongs on vowel diagrams by adding an arrow to show the direction of the glide from the starting point of the vowel (see Fig. 4.2).

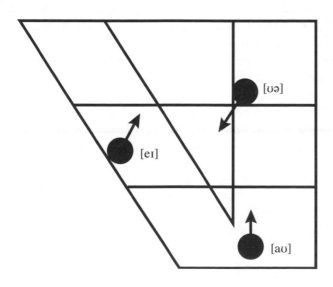

4.2
Vowel diagram showing selected SBE diphthongs

VOWEL VARIATION

Short
Long

We have now met with three kinds of English vowel: SHORT monoph-thongs, like [e] in *head* or [ɪ] in *hid*, LONG monophthongs, such as [ɑː] of *father*, and (another variety of LONG vowel) diphthongs like [ɔɪ] of *voice*. Although accents of English tend to have essentially the same set of consonants, they differ much more widely in the vowels they employ. For that reason, we can't hope to cover all the ways that your own speech may be different from that described above. Your own vowels will usually be sufficiently similar overall to make it possible for you to understand the distinction between monophthong and diphthong, and the basic dimensions of vowel quality description.

All kinds of English have both monophthongs and diphthongs, but they do not agree precisely on which words will contain them. For instance, *say* and *go* have diphthongs in SBE ([eɪ] and [əʊ] respectively) but monophthongs in Scottish accents and in many accents from the North of England. The Scottish vowels can be written [eː] and [oː]. If you have a rhotic accent, you may not have the diphthongs [ɪə], [eə] and [ʊə], but a monophthong followed by [r]. Another big difference is over the vowel [ʌ] we have shown in *cup*, *love*, etc. Half of England lacks this vowel – all the Midlands and the North, in fact. Generally [ʊ] is used in all those words where the South has the additional vowel [ʌ]; so *Hudd* is a homophone of *hood*, and *putt* is the same as *put*.

SUMMARY

- Vowel quality – how a vowel sounds – is a function of the combina-tion of the part of the tongue being used (front–central–back), how near or far this is from the palate (high–mid–low) and lip position (spread–neutral–rounded).
- Vowels may be pronounced with longer or shorter duration, with a single quality (monophthongs) or with a glide from one quality to another (diphthongs).
- In utterances of more than one syllable, some syllables will be more prominent than others and these are said to be stressed.
- Unstressed syllables frequently contain the vowel schwa in English.

FURTHER EXERCISES

4.6 Read and identify the following words, giving the orthographic (spelling) forms.

1. ['eksəsaızız]
2. [ə'griːmənt]
3. ['tʃaıldıʃnəs]
4. [dɪsəd'vaːntɪdʒ]
5. [fɔː'tɪsɪməʊ]
6. [ɪntɒksɪ'keıʃn]
7. [lʌk'ʃʊərɪəs]
8. [rɪ'kluːs]
9. [ɪ'kwɪvələns]
10. [rɪ'kwaɪəmənt]

4.7 Using all the pairs of words given in Exercises 4.1 and 4.3, compare the two vowels in terms of front–back.

4.8 The English sounds [w] and [j] are sometimes called SEMI-VOWELS, meaning that they are in some ways like vowels. Which two vowels do [w] and [j] seem to resemble, and why? How would you demonstrate that despite their resemblance to vowels the two sounds should be counted as consonants within the English sound system?

Semi-vowel

4.9 Transcribe the phrase *Where were you a year ago?* and make a detailed description of the rounding and unrounding of the lips, using drawings and diagrams. (Observe yourself in a mirror – or, if you have access to a video camera, record one or more speakers and stop the motion to sketch what you see.)

5

THE ORGANS OF SPEECH AND PLACE OF ARTICULATION

In this chapter, we will introduce you to the organs of speech and to the concept of place of articulation of consonants. (We recommend you to work through this chapter with a small mirror beside you to check the correspondence between the description of sounds and what you can see.)

ORGANS OF SPEECH

Organs of speech

The ORGANS OF SPEECH are all parts of the body that serve other primary biological purposes: breathing, biting, chewing, licking, swallowing, etc. You can see from this that we are referring especially to the lungs and to parts of the body in what we call in everyday English the mouth and throat. Except to note that they are the main 'reservoir' of air used in speech production, the lungs need not concern us further here. The mouth and throat, known as the supra-glottal VOCAL TRACT, are where we need to focus.

Vocal tract

Look carefully at Figure 5.1. This is a vocal tract diagram (or, more technically, a SAGITTAL CROSS-SECTION). You can probably see that it is a drawing of a head chopped in half!

Sagittal cross-section

If we trace the passage of air being expelled from the speaker's lungs (called the egressive pulmonic airstream), we will find the first so-called speech organ it encounters at the base of the diagram, the larynx (where the vocal folds are located). This is where voice is produced. When the folds are held open (as for quiet breathing or for the production of voiceless speech sounds) the space between them is called the GLOTTIS.

Glottis

Egressive pulmonic air continues out through the glottis and into the spaces or cavities above, the supra-glottal cavities which together form the supra-glottal vocal tract. It is the glottis, by the way, that gives us

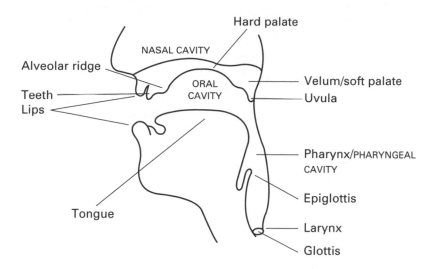

Hard palate

NASAL CAVITY

Alveolar ridge

ORAL CAVITY

Velum/soft palate

Teeth
Lips

Uvula

Pharynx/PHARYNGEAL CAVITY

Epiglottis

Tongue

Larynx

Glottis

5.1 The vocal tract

the name of the 'glottal stop' – an obstruction to the free passage of air caused by closing the glottis. GLOTTAL is therefore the name of a place of articulation. Supra-glottal (*supra* = 'above') means anything in the vocal tract above the glottis.

Glottal

Immediately above the glottis is an irregular tube-like cavity which for speech purposes we call by its anatomical name, the PHARYNX. It is the pharynx to which we refer in colloquial usage as the throat.

Pharynx

At the top of the pharynx are two more major cavities: the ORAL CAVITY (the mouth) and the NASAL CAVITY (all the interconnecting chambers within the nose, more properly called the nasal cavities). Access for egressive pulmonic air to the oral cavity is open at all times during speech, but access to the nasal cavity is controlled by the valve-like behaviour of an organ called the VELUM. The velum is capable of opening (lowering) and closing (raising) like a trapdoor, enabling or preventing the passage of egressive pulmonic air into the nasal cavity. When it is raised and the air cannot enter the nasal cavity, we say there is VELIC CLOSURE (see Fig. 5.2).

Oral cavity
Nasal cavity

Velum

Velic closure

The nasal cavity need not concern us further here. It has no moving parts and nothing further to contribute to speech production beyond being coupled into the network of supra-glottal cavities for the production of certain sounds and closed off for others.

The most important space by far is the oral cavity. Here it helps to make a basic distinction between organs that can move and which can be called ACTIVE ARTICULATORS and organs which cannot move and which can be called PASSIVE ARTICULATORS. It is the inherent relationship between these that establishes the names of PLACES OF ARTICULATION.

Active articulator
Passive articulator
Place of articulation

Moveable organs include the LIPS, lower jaw and, the most flexible organ of all, the TONGUE (see Fig. 5.3). Because of its extreme flexibility,

Lip
Tongue

5.2 Velic closure

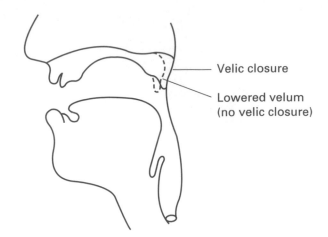

Velic closure

Lowered velum
(no velic closure)

5.3 Parts of the tongue

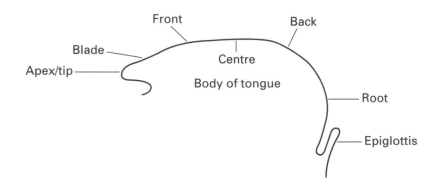

Front

Back

Blade

Centre

Apex/tip

Body of tongue

Root

Epiglottis

the tongue is typically divided up into parts, each capable of (relatively) independent movement. Have a mirror handy to look at your own tongue and compare what you can see with the above diagram.

EXERCISE

Apex
Apical

Blade

Front

Back

5.1 Stick your tongue out. You can see that it ends in a sort of point. This is called the tip or APEX. Articulations made by movements of this part of the tongue are called APICAL. The apex is the termination of the free section of the tongue, unattached by any kind of membrane or tissue to the lower jaw, called the BLADE. Immediately behind that, but still clearly visible, at the point at which you begin to notice the tongue being attached to the lower jaw, is the part we call the FRONT. And behind the front, still just visible in your mirror, is the BACK. You will notice that the moveability or flexibility of the tongue decreases as you move further in towards the back of the mouth, but the least flexible section of all is actually hidden from your view where the tongue ROOT forms the front wall of the pharynx.

Root

In Figure 5.3, you will also notice one other organ at this point. Not widely used in speech production, the EPIGLOTTIS is the organ primarily responsible for preventing foreign bodies (solids and liquids) from entering the lungs when we swallow.

Epiglottis

At the intersection between the front and back of the tongue is a location which can be usefully referred to as the CENTRE. Movements made with parts of the tongue between the blade and centre are called LAMINAL and between the back and centre, DORSAL.

Centre
Laminal
Dorsal

EXERCISE

5.2 Again, use your mirror so that you can look into your mouth and see what you can see. Moving from left to right in the diagram (Fig. 5.1) we can identify the relevant organs. The lips we have already mentioned. Behind them are the lower front incisors and the upper front incisors, called TEETH in the diagram, which contribute to speech production. If you run the tip of your tongue up the back of your upper front teeth and on to the roof of your mouth you will feel it passing over a hard 'bump' or ridge. This is the ALVEOLAR RIDGE. Continuing beyond the ridge, your tongue tip will feel a concavity or depression, still with a hard surface, which is part of the PALATE called the HARD PALATE. If you have a very flexible tongue, you may be able to feel further back still and notice a position at which the hard surface gives way to a soft one. The palate is in two parts, the hard palate (called 'palate' above) and the SOFT PALATE. In speech production, we call the soft palate the VELUM.

Teeth

Alveolar ridge

Palate
Hard palate

Soft palate
Velum

In your mirror, it may be difficult to see the alveolar ridge, but you will be able to see the concave surface of the palate. You will also be able to see the pendulous termination of the soft part of this organ – the little wriggly organ which is visible hanging down at the back of your mouth. This is the UVULA.

Uvula

Beyond the uvula, the vocal tract turns a corner, down into the pharynx, and becomes invisible. The only significant locations here are the two we have already met, the pharynx itself and the glottis.

PLACE OF ARTICULATION

Now study the diagram (Fig. 5.1) again. It shows a speaker with the mouth a little open, but otherwise at rest. (With the mouth closed and the jaw lightly clenched, we would call this the REST POSITION.)

Rest position

EXERCISE

5.3 Close your mouth and swallow slowly and thoughtfully. Concentrate on what you can feel of the relationship between the surface of the tongue and the roof of the mouth. How does what you feel match the following description?

Comment

You will notice that, at rest, the parts of the lower jaw and tongue line up naturally with different parts of the roof of the mouth: lower lip to upper lip and teeth; tip and blade of tongue to teeth and alveolar ridge; front of tongue to hard palate; back of tongue to velum and uvula; root of tongue to back wall of the pharynx. These established inherent relationships mean that, unless anything steps out of line (and the only thing flexible enough to do this, really, is the tip/blade section of the tongue) or if we want to be especially precise, it is not necessary to refer to the active articulator every time we mention a place of articulation. So, when the two lips articulate together (and you can see this happening twice if you look in your mirror and say *baby*) or the lower lip articulates with the teeth (and you can see this happening twice if you look in your mirror and say *fever*) we can say that all the consonant sounds being produced are LABIAL.

Labial

The fact of the matter is that we do often need to distinguish between these two different kind of labial gestures (we would need to do this when describing consonant sounds in English, for example) and so we have two rather more precise place names for this purpose: BILABIAL ('both lips' for the consonants in *baby*) and LABIODENTAL ('lip and teeth' for the consonants in *fever*).

Bilabial
Labiodental

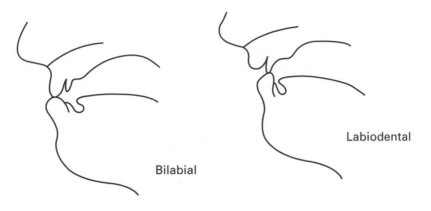

5.4 Bilabial and labiodental adjustments in vocal tract diagrams

Labiodental

Bilabial

The lips and teeth in our sagittal sections or vocal tract drawings can be adjusted to show these postures (see Fig. 5.4).

Sometimes, two places of articulation are operated at the same time. This is the case in English [w], for example. You can see the lips are involved, but at the same time, the back of your tongue is making a movement (which although you can't see it you may be able to feel a bit) towards the velum. [w] therefore has a sort of double-barrelled name: LABIAL–VELAR. DOUBLE ARTICULATIONS of this kind are rare, but to use two places at once is a recognized way of increasing the number of different sounds we are capable of producing.

Labial–velar
Double articulation

EXERCISES

5.4 Do not use the Table 5.1 for this exercise, but look at the diagrams in Figures 5.1 and 5.3. Then, relying on these diagrams and your new knowledge of the inherent relationships between active and passive articulators, work out what active articulator(s) are most likely to be used if a sound is made at the following places of articulation:

1. dental	2. velar	3. palatal
4. labiodental	5. uvular	6. alveolar
7. labial–palatal	8. bilabial	

5.5 Again, use the diagrams in Figures 5.1 and 5.3 above and not Table 5.1. Relying on the same knowledge, what would the passive articulator(s) be if the following active articulators were used?

1. front of tongue
2. lower lip

3. tongue tip
4. lower lip and back of tongue
5. blade and front of tongue
6. blade of tongue

5.6

(a) What do you judge to be the active and passive articulators involved in the production of the consonant sound at the beginning of each of the following English words? Use your mirror and the knowledge you have gained from the previous exercises in this chapter.

1. boy	2. think	3. very	4. five
5. guess	6. yes	7. car	8. tea
9. light	10. pen	11. next	12. say
13. zip	14. then	15. do	16. psychic
17. written	18. mnemonic		

(b) Now, refer to Table 5.1 to establish the names of the places of articulation that are given to each of these gestures and the sounds they produce.

Comment

Table 5.1 summarizes the main active–passive relationships at the various places of articulation and introduces the full range of place names. You will see that it is possible to distinguish at least eleven single or PRIMARY ARTICULATIONS and two or three double articulations. As you will see, there are some places of articulation that English does not use. This will be true in the case of any language.

Primary articulation

When this information is put together with what you already know about voicing, we have the beginning of the phonetic system for consonant description. This is a three-part labelling system which enables us to give a unique name or description for any consonant sound that a speaker might make. The first two parts of each label give information about the voicing of the sound and its place of articulation.

Table 5.1 *Places of articulation*

Articulators		Place name	Examples
Passive: Active:	Upper lip Lower lip	Bilabial	[p b m]
Passive: Active:	Upper front teeth Lower lip	Labiodental	[f v]
Passive: Active:	Upper front teeth Tongue tip or blade	Dental	[θ ð]
Passive: Active:	Alveolar ridge Tongue tip or blade	Alveolar	[t d n s z l]
Passive: Active:	Back of alveolar ridge Tongue tip	Postalveolar	[ɹ] (= /r/)
Passive: Active:	Front of hard palate Underside of tongue tip	Retroflex (= apico-palatal)	American English 'r': [ɻ]
Passive: Active:	Back of alveolar ridge, front of hard palate Blade of tongue and front of tongue	Palatoalveolar (a subset of the postalveolar group)	[ʃ ʒ tʃ dʒ]
Passive: Active:	Hard palate Front of (body of) tongue	Palatal	[j]
Passive: Active:	Velum (= soft palate) Back of (body of) tongue	Velar	[k g ŋ]
Passive: Active:	Uvula Back of (body of) tongue	Uvular	French 'r': [ʁ]
Passive: Active:	(Back wall of) pharynx Root of tongue	Pharyngeal	Arabic 'ayn': [ʕ]
Passive: Active:	– Vocal folds	Glottal	[h ʔ]
Passive: Active:	Upper lip, velum Lower lip, back of tongue	Labial–velar	[w]
Passive: Active:	Upper lip, hard palate Lower lip, front of tongue	Labial–palatal	French [ɥ] as in *lui* [lɥi]

SUMMARY

- The organs of speech give their names to the places of articulation.
- Places of articulation are the static or passive points on the upper surface of the oral cavity towards which the active articulators (lower lip and the tongue) move in the production of speech sounds.
- There is an inherent relationship (apparent through study of the alignment of organs in the rest position) between active and passive articulators which means that it is not necessary to mention the active articulator every time we name or label a speech sound.
- The name of the place of articulation supplies the second term in the three-term labelling system for consonants – the first recognizes whether the sound is voiced or voiceless.
- The principle places of articulation are summarized and illustrated in Table 5.1.

FURTHER EXERCISES

5.7   Here are all the English consonants:

[p t k b d g f θ s ʃ h v ð z ʒ tʃ dʒ m n ŋ w ɹ l j]

(a)   Divide them into two groups, putting all the voiceless ones together and all the voiced ones together.

(b)   Fill the items from each group into the following matrix:

Place of articulation	Voiceless sounds	Voiced sounds
Bilabial		
Labiodental		
Dental		
Alveolar		
Postalveolar		
Palatoalveolar		
Palatal		
Velar		
Glottal		
Labial–velar		

5.8 Give three examples of English words beginning with the following consonant sounds:

1. voiced bilabial
2. voiceless alveolar
3. voiced labial–velar
4. voiced labiodental
5. voiceless palatoalveolar
6. voiced palatal
7. voiceless bilabial
8. voiceless velar
9. voiceless dental
10. voiced postalveolar

5.9 Give three examples of words ending with the following sounds:

1. voiced bilabial
2. voiceless alveolar
3. voiced velar
4. voiced labiodental
5. voiceless palatoalveolar
6. voiced alveolar
7. voiceless bilabial
8. voiceless velar
9. voiceless dental
10. voiceless labiodental

5.10 As well as identifying consonant sounds with articulatory labels, we can represent them in diagrams. What do you judge to be the place of articulation of each of the following consonants? (In each case look carefully to determine which active articulators are involved and which passive articulator they are relating to.)

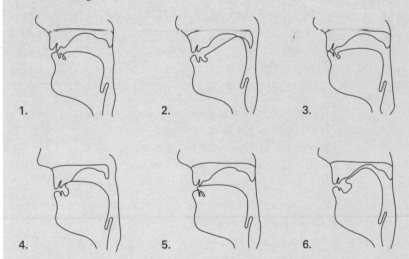

1.   2.   3.

4.   5.   6.

5.11 Phoneticians also need to be able to draw these diagrams quickly and easily. Complete the diagrams on the following page to illustrate an articulation at each of the six different places of articulation given.

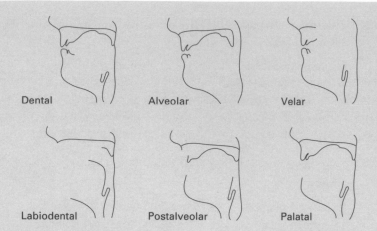

Dental   Alveolar   Velar

Labiodental   Postalveolar   Palatal

5.12 Give voice and place labels to each of the consonants in the following utterances. Begin by transcribing them.

1. Try to be very quick.
2. It's fairly easy, once you know how.
3. Judge the voicing first.
4. Nearly finished!
5. Check the answers carefully.

5.13

(a) Look at the Dyirbal data on p. 11. Make a list of the consonants and organize them into voiceless and voiced groups and by place of articulation. (Try to make a table of the sort used in Exercise 5.7 above.)

(b) Look at any page and answer the following questions:

1. How many voiced consonants can you find?
2. How many voiceless consonants can you find?
3. How many bilabial consonants can you find?
4. How many velar consonants can you find?
5. How many alveolar consonants can you find?

(Remember that when we use the term consonant, we are talking about consonant sounds, *not* spellings!)

(c) If you enjoy counting data, you can repeat exercise (b) for any text you choose. You could look for other places of articulation, too.

5.14 How many places of articulation are used in English? Do we find voiced and voiceless consonants at all of these places? If not, which ones are 'voiced only' and which 'voiceless only'?

MANNER OF ARTICULATION AND AIRSTREAM MECHANISMS 6

> In this chapter, we will introduce the concepts of manner of articulation and airstream mechanisms.

MANNER OF ARTICULATION

If you look at your answers to Exercises 5.7 or 5.13(a) in the previous chapter, you will see that we are well on the way to being able to give a unique label to each and every speech sound that humans can make. In English, using voice and place descriptions only, we can identify [j] as a voiced palatal and [ɹ] as a voiced postalveolar and [w] as a voiced labial–velar. Other groups have only two members, and these also can now be identified distinctively within the system: voiceless dental [θ], for example, and voiced dental [ð]. However, as soon as we start to look at sounds made at the bilabial or velar place, we can already see that these two-part labels are inadequate, and the alveolar place with its six different sounds confirms this!

The next step, then, is to consider the MANNER in which each of these sounds is made. In doing this, we are looking more closely at two related aspects of each sound: first, we are considering what it actually sounds like, the 'sound effect' if you like; and second, we are looking at the type of gesture that is responsible for making such a sound. **Manner**

Just as there turned out to be quite a large number of possible places of articulation, so we will discover there is a range of different manners. The inclusion of manner information in the labelling system will then enable us to create the kinds of distinctive labels we need to identify each sound separately.

A large number of manner contrasts are produced by interfering in different ways with the egressive pulmonic airstream that we use most of the time when speaking. This is the case in most languages. In some languages, however, a number of more exotic contrasts are brought about by using air contained in cavities other than the lungs and by varying the direction of flow for this air (making it ingressive instead of egressive).

ORAL, NASAL AND NASALIZED

The first major distinction that needs to be made concerns the route taken by the air flowing out from the lungs. When we described the organs of speech, you may remember that we looked at the behaviour of the velum and described the way in which it was capable of directing the airflow. The velum acted like a valve or door, moving down to create an opening through which air could enter the nasal cavity or being held in the raised position, closing the nasal cavity off and only permitting airflow into the mouth.

Oral

For the great majority of speech sounds, the velum is held in the raised position, forming velic closure (see Fig. 6.1) and permitting air to flow only into the mouth. Sounds created with this kind of airflow are known collectively as ORAL speech sounds. There are a great many such sounds and we will need to make a more detailed study of what happens to air going through the mouth in order to distinguish between them. We can show oral airflow in a vocal tract drawing by adding airflow arrows.

When there is no velic closure, however, we have one of two possible situations. It may be that the oral cavity is closed or totally obstructed at some point. You can see an obstruction of this kind at the lips if you look in your mirror and say words like *papa, baby, mummy*. In the case of the last of these, together with the oral obstruction, the air is permitted

Nasal

to flow through the nasal cavity, producing what we describe as a NASAL

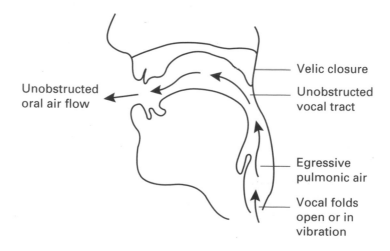

Velic closure

Unobstructed oral air flow

Unobstructed vocal tract

Egressive pulmonic air

Vocal folds open or in vibration

6.1 Unobstructed oral airflow

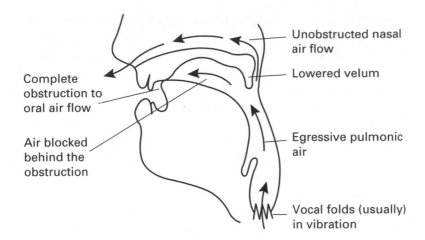

6.2 Nasal airflow

Unobstructed nasal air flow

Lowered velum

Complete obstruction to oral air flow

Air blocked behind the obstruction

Egressive pulmonic air

Vocal folds (usually) in vibration

manner of sound. The oral obstruction can be 'at any place of articulation in the oral cavity (see Fig. 6.2, for example, which shows a complete obstruction at the alveolar ridge)..

EXERCISE

6.1 To check the direction of airflow, try saying *mummy* while pinching your nostrils shut – you will get something that sounds much more like *bubby*! Now do the same thing for the word *nanny*. What other English word does it remind you of when you pinch your nostrils?

So, [m] and [n] are both nasal consonants, while [b] and [d] are some kind of oral sound. Has English got any other nasals?

This is one of the possibilities, then: oral airflow blocked at some point in the mouth but free nasal airflow, resulting in the production of nasal consonants.

However, in situations where the velum is in the lowered position and there is no obstruction in the oral cavity, it is also possible to have simultaneous nasal and oral airflow. This produces the effect we call NASALIZATION (see Fig. 6.3). Nasalization can affect the way some consonants sound, but it is especially important in connection with vowels. In the English word *man*, for example, the velum, which has to be in the lowered position for both the [m] and the [n], in fact stays in

Nasalization

Nasalized vowel

that position all the way through. This results in the production of a so-called NASALIZED VOWEL, [æ̃]. (Nasalization is transcribed by placing the diacritic [˜] above the relevant vowel or consonant symbol.) Although the tongue and the jaw and the lips are all in exactly the same position as they would be for the [æ] in the middle of *bad*, there is no velic closure and so the vowel acquires an additional nasalized resonance from the simultaneous free passage of air through the nasal cavity. In English, this always tends to happen when vowels are next to nasal consonants and people don't even notice it when they are listening to the language being spoken because it never means anything particular, never changes the meaning of what is being said. In a language like French, however, the velum is lowered deliberately in certain vowel sounds to produce a nasalized vowel instead of an oral vowel and this has the effect of changing the meaning of the word. French has four nasalized vowels which are demonstrated in the famous phrase *un bon vin blanc* (a good white wine) [œ̃ bɔ̃ vɛ̃ blɑ̃]. Each of these vowels can contrast with a related oral vowel, for example *très* (very) [tʀɛ] but *train* (train) [tʀɛ̃] and *bas* (low) [bɑ] but *banc* (bench) [bɑ̃]. From the transcriptions, you can see that French signals the presence of a nasalized vowel in its spelling by the letter *n* after the vowel letter, but the *n* is like some of the silent letters we have seen in English spelling and is not itself pronounced when the words are spoken aloud.

Parametric diagram

Apart from showing the velum raised or lowered in vocal tract drawings, phoneticians also sometimes represent this movement of the velum in what are called PARAMETRIC DIAGRAMS (see Fig. 6.4). We can use a series of such diagrams to represent the difference in velum action in the words *bad, ban, man, mad*, for example. You will need to practise diagrams of this kind.

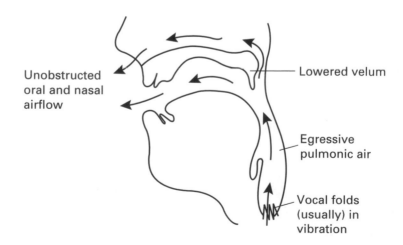

Unobstructed oral and nasal airflow

Lowered velum

Egressive pulmonic air

Vocal folds (usually) in vibration

6.3 Nasalized airflow

Velum action:
raised/closed

lowered/open

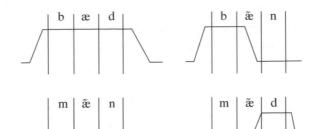

EXERCISES

6.2 Following the above examples of velum action diagrams, draw the equivalent diagrams for each of the following utterances:

1. comb	2. thin	3. singing	4. gnat
5. umbrella	6. brother	7. runny	8. incline
9. complaint	10. invention	11. wish	12. tomato

6.3 Look at the following parametric diagrams illustrating velum action and give an English word for which each could be true. To help you, C = consonant (other than a nasal consonant), V = any vowel, N = any nasal.

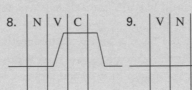

6.4 Start keeping a list of full phonetic labels (voice–place–manner labels) for the English consonants, beginning with [m n] and [ŋ].

6.5 Can you say what is happening in the following anonymous verse?

> Chilly Dovebber with his boadigg blast
> Dow cubs add strips the bedow add the lawd.
>
> (Chilly November with its moaning blast, / Now comes and strips the meadow and the lawn.)

The title of the poem means 'Melancholy days'. The author wrote it in such a way that it suggested the same problem – how do you think it was spelled? Under what circumstances would you expect to sound like this?

So, as well as studying some general characteristics of airflow in sound production, we have now established the first manner label for consonants, nasal.

AIRSTREAM MECHANISMS

Paralinguistic sound

A small number of world languages use air other than lung air to make consonant sounds, and at least a few of these sounds are familiar to us as speakers of English because, although we don't use them as a regular part of our everyday speech, we use them as PARALINGUISTIC SOUNDS to convey special socially recognized meanings. Examples of these include the sound of disapproval which novelists often seem to spell out as *tut! tut!*, the sound we make when we want to encourage a horse to get moving, the 'gee-up sound' which involves a sort of sucking in of air at the side of the mouth, the sound we make when we want to imitate the noise made by horses' hooves (sort of 'clip-clop sound') and the sound we make when we kiss with our lips. If you cannot think what these might sound like for yourself, talk to a few friends and see what they can come up with.

By far the biggest group of these rather exotic sounds are made using air contained in the pharynx which is pushed out of the vocal tract under pressure by rapid raising of the larynx with the glottis firmly closed. This upward movement of the larynx occurs simultaneously with the production of a plosive, fricative or affricate manner of articulation in the oral

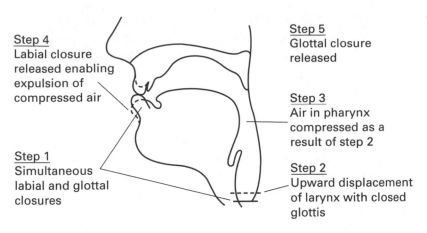

Step 4
Labial closure
released enabling
expulsion of
compressed air

Step 5
Glottal closure
released

Step 3
Air in pharynx
compressed as a
result of step 2

Step 1
Simultaneous
labial and glottal
closures

Step 2
Upward displacement
of larynx with closed
glottis

6.5 Sequence of movements in the production of [p']

cavity (Fig. 6.5). The extremely rapid expulsion of this relatively small quantity of air gives all sounds made this way a very short duration resulting in a very staccato effect. It is often said that they sound 'dart-like', as if they are being 'spat out', giving a very short and sharp auditory impression compared with their ordinary pulmonic egressive counterparts.

This AIRSTREAM MECHANISM has two names, both current and equally correct. It is known either as the egressive pharyngeal airstream mechanism (deriving from the name of the cavity in which the air is contained) or the egressive GLOTTALIC airstream mechanism (deriving from the name of the organ that sets the air moving).

Airstream mechanism

Glottalic

The necessary presence of a glottal stop (which enables the larynx to act a bit like the piston in a bicycle pump) means that all these sounds, called EJECTIVE consonants, are voiceless. The glottal stop is represented in diacritic form in the symbols used to transcribe these sounds which are essentially the routine pulmonic egressive symbol like [p f tʃ] but followed immediately by a little raised comma (a small version of the cursive top of the glottal stop symbol), [p' f' tʃ'] symbolizing respectively a voiceless bilabial ejective plosive, a voiceless labiodental ejective fricative and a voiceless palatoalveolar ejective affricate.

Ejective

If you are beginning to gain some control over your articulatory organs (like switching voice off and on at will, deliberately raising and lowering the velum, etc.) you may be able to produce these sounds for yourself.

EXERCISE

6.6 Breathe out until there is no air left in your lungs at all and then try to say [p t k p t k p t k] over and over until you have to breathe in. If you succeed in producing a series of sharp, short 'dart-like' sounds, you have probably succeeded in producing ejective plosives.

Ejective forms of the plosives, fricatives and affricates are the forms taught to people who have undergone the surgical removal of their larynx and who can no longer use lung air to speak. Some normal speakers also use ejective plosives for stylistic effect, perhaps adding a certain emphasis, when they say things like *quite!* [kwaɪt'].

In world language terms, ejectives are the most widespread of all the non-pulmonic consonants and are found in African languages like Amharic and Tigre (spoken in Ethiopia), Zulu (spoken in South Africa), Hausa (spoken in Nigeria) and Caucasian languages like Georgian. They are especially characteristic of American Indian languages from all over the continent like Chipewyan, Dakota, Navaho, Nez Perce, Nootka, Quechua and Squamish, to name but a few.

The direction of airflow for ejectives was seen to be outward, egressive, but the same body of air – the air in the pharynx – can also be made to move inwards by making a sudden downward displacement of the larynx. This works by fractionally enlarging the space in the pharynx which gives the air more room and so causes the air pressure to drop. If this movement is made to occur simultaneously with the release of a complete closure further forward in the vocal tract, somewhere in the oral cavity, because the pressure inside the tract is then lower than the ambient air pressure (the pressure outside the speaker, in front of the place of obstruction), that air (the ambient air) is sucked into the vocal tract to make the two pressures equal. This results in a sort of gulping noise and the sounds produced this way are called IMPLOSIVE consonants and symbolized, for example, [ɓ ɗ ɠ] (see Fig. 6.6). When displaced downwards, the larynx will usually be vibrating, giving rise to the production of voiced implosives.

Implosive

As for ejectives, there are two names for the airstream mechanism which is this time prefixed by ingressive, indicating the drawing in of air into the vocal tract: ingressive pharyngeal airstream mechanism or ingressive glottalic airstream mechanism.

Sometimes people make a kind of implosive noise when they are imitating the sound of liquids being poured out of a narrow-necked bottle, but there is no regular social or stylistic application of these by English speakers to which we can refer you.

Implosives are much less widespread than ejectives. They are found especially in African languages, including the more well-known Zulu,

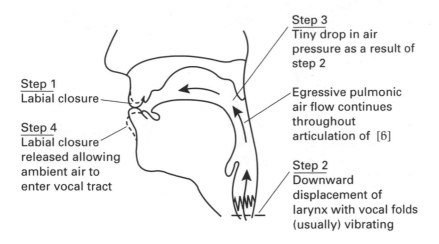

Step 3
Tiny drop in air
pressure as a result of
step 2

Step 1
Labial closure

Step 4
Labial closure
released allowing
ambient air to
enter vocal tract

Egressive pulmonic
air flow continues
throughout
articulation of [ɓ]

Step 2
Downward
displacement of
larynx with vocal folds
(usually) vibrating

6.6 Sequence of
movements in the
production of [ɓ]

Swahili, Hausa, Igbo and Maasai. Implosives are also reported for Vietnamese and Khmer.

Finally, the least widespread of all the non-pulmonics, but often the best known because of the famous 'click song' (popularized by Miriam Makeba) and the musical *Ipi Tombi*, are the CLICK consonants. **Click**

Clicks are made using oral air, air contained in the oral cavity. First, it is necessary to create a completely sealed chamber in the mouth. This is done by making a complete velar closure (like for [k g ŋ]) at the back of the mouth and then some other closure more forward than this, bilabial, alveolar or postalveolar, for example. Then, by hollowing the front of the tongue as much as possible, this chamber or container full of air is made bigger, causing the pressure of the air in it (which now has more space) to decrease. After that, the effect is very similar to the one described for implosives. Having reduced the pressure inside the cavity, when the forward closure is removed, the ambient air (the outside air) which is now higher in pressure is sucked into the mouth to equalize the two pressures. The result this time is a click sound (see Fig. 6.7).

Clicks have reasonable currency as paralinguistic characteristics of speech in English and, as such, were described above on p. 50. The sounds referred to there are respectively a voiceless dental click (the *tut! tut!* noise) [k͡ǀ] a voiceless alveolar lateral click (the gee-up noise) [k͡ǁ], a voiceless postalveolar click (horses' hooves) [k͡ǃ] and a voiceless bilabial click (kissing) [k͡ʘ]. Note that voicelessness in clicks is indicated by coupling the basic symbol to the voiceless velar plosive symbol (remember that a k-sound is actually being made at the same time as the more audible, percussive click gesture – read the account of the mechanism again if you are unsure).

The airstream mechanism involved here again has two names, one deriving from the cavity in which the air is contained, the ingressive oral airstream mechanism, the other from the initiator, the organ which sets

6.7 Sequence of movements in the production of [k͡ʘ]

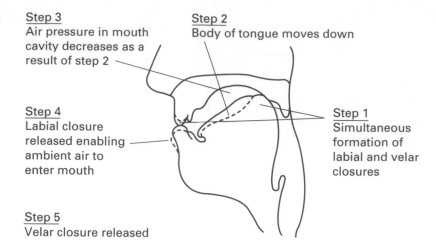

Step 3
Air pressure in mouth cavity decreases as a result of step 2

Step 2
Body of tongue moves down

Step 4
Labial closure released enabling ambient air to enter mouth

Step 1
Simultaneous formation of labial and velar closures

Step 5
Velar closure released

Velaric

the air in motion which in this case is the gesture of velar closure, giving ingressive VELARIC airstream mechanism. Because the principal articulatory gesture is entirely independent of both the larynx and the velum (as valve), clicks may be voiceless as we have described them here, voiced, or voiced and nasalized. Voiced clicks are transcribed by coupling the symbol with a voiced velar plosive, hence [g͡ǃ] for a voiced postalveolar or retroflex click and voiced nasalized clicks by coupling the symbol to a voiced velar nasal, hence [ŋ͡ǃ] for a voiced nasalized postalveolar click. Ejective consonants involve air being forced out of the vocal tract – pushed out under pressure; these sounds are sometimes referred to as

Pressure consonant

PRESSURE CONSONANTS. Implosives and clicks, however, involve air being drawn into the vocal tract (ingressive air-flow); these sounds can

Suction consonant

be termed SUCTION CONSONANTS.

SUMMARY

- Manner of articulation is the name given to the type of sound (relating to its auditory effect and the way in which this effect is created); it is the third term in the consonant labelling system, VOICE–PLACE–MANNER LABELS (or VPM LABELS).

Voice–place–manner labels VPM labels

- Nasal sounds are produced with the velum lowered giving free passage of air through the nasal cavity and with oral airflow completely obstructed; oral sounds have free oral airflow but velic closure; nasalized sounds have free airflow simultaneously through both cavities.

- Further variety is achieved by the use of different airstream mechanisms in addition to the usual pulmonic egressive one, these are: egressive glottalic or pharyngeal (producing ejectives, a type of pressure consonant), ingressive glottalic or pharyngeal (producing implosives, a type of suction consonant) and ingressive velaric or oral (producing clicks, another type of suction consonant).

FURTHER EXERCISES

6.7 1. Give six examples of words ending in each of the three English nasal consonants.

2. Can you find all three of these sounds at the beginning of words in English? Give three examples of each word-initial nasal.

3. Give three examples of each nasal occurring in the middle of a word.

6.8 The author Ngaio Marsh comes from New Zealand. Judging from the spelling, what sound do you think her name might begin with in Maori? How do English people pronounce the name Ngaio?

6.9

> Now and again, a freak distribution turns up. You might be dealt all the spades, or all the aces, kings, queens and the odd jack. You could then call seven spades or seven no trumps. But such manna from heaven doesn't fall more than once in a lifetime, and for the most part, Contract Bridge is a game of skill.
>
> (From *Waddingtons Family Card Games*
> by Robert Harbin)

1. Transcribe all the words containing a voiced alveolar nasal. How many such consonants are there in this passage?

2. Make a transcribed list of all the words containing a voiced velar nasal.

3. Go through the passage and indicate the nasalized vowels by placing the nasalization diacritic above them.

6.10 Draw and label a vocal tract diagram for each of the English nasal consonants. (You can indicate voice in the larynx by use of a zigzag line: VVVV. Voicelessness can be shown by an empty circle.)

7 CONSONANT DESCRIPTION AND VOICE–PLACE–MANNER LABELS

In this chapter, we will complete the study of manner of articulation and practise the application of full phonetic labels, often called voice–place–manner labels and abbreviated to VPM labels.

ORAL MANNERS OF ARTICULATION

Clearly, glancing again at our entry for English alveolar consonants ([t d n s z l]) we can see that there are still going to be quite a large number of different types or manners of speech sounds to identify if we are going to be able to give distinctive three-part phonetic labels to each of the consonants in this set.

The best way to approach the different manners of oral consonants is to group them first according to how much of a gap there is between the active and passive articulators. (There will still be some sounds left over even when we have done this, but this is a good first step.)

Think again about how the nasals were articulated. The active and passive articulators formed a complete obstruction to the airstream and so they were firmly in contact with each other. If this same gesture is made, but this time with the velum in the raised position so that we also have velic closure, we get the first major class of oral consonants. To produce these consonants, the active articulator approaches the passive one, contacts it and forms a firm closure; even while this closure is in place, air is still being expelled from the lungs; but there is also velic closure and so the only place for air to go is into the mouth, as far as the obstruction; this causes air pressure in the mouth to build up; after a brief interval of 'holding' this position, the active articulator moves sharply away from the passive one, creating a fairly wide gap between them (which we call wide MEDIAN APPROXIMATION) and allowing all

Median approximation

the air to explode out of the oral cavity; we hear this as a sort of single burst or pop or explosive sound and this is how we make sounds like the consonants in the middle of *appear* and *obey*, at the beginning of *pay* and *bang* and at the end of *hope* and *hob*. Such sounds are called PLOSIVE. Thus we have a voiceless bilabial plosive in *appear*, *pay*, *hope* and a voiced bilabial plosive in *obey*, *bang*, *hob*. If we add to these the voiced bilabial nasal at the beginning of *me*, you can see that our system is already capable of distinguishing all the English bilabials.

Plosive

EXERCISES

7.1 Try to find more plosives among the English consonants. Add them to your list, together with the symbol and a keyword in each case. (There are five more altogether including the glottal stop for which we now have the full phonetic label voiceless glottal plosive.)

Think of English words which give six more examples of each sound.

7.2 1. Circle the words that end with a plosive. (Remember to keep thinking about sounds – don't be distracted by the spelling.)

batch	stack	dumb	wrong
sink	tomb	end	lump
crab	loch	gnat	log

2. Circle the words that begin with a plosive.

pick	knit	chin	dump
glue	chemist	physics	tree
psychic	George	ptarmigan	bread

We can draw a diagram to illustrate the three main phases of plosive articulation (Fig. 7.1): the APPROACH PHASE (the active articulator moving towards the passive one), the HOLD PHASE (the duration of the closure between the two articulators) and the RELEASE PHASE (the separating of the articulators with the accompanying audible 'plosion').

Approach phase
Hold phase
Release phase

If we keep thinking in terms of pairs of active and passive articulators and now imagine that instead of forming a complete closure, the active articulator stops short just before it presses firmly against the passive one, leaving only the lightest of contacts or even a very narrow gap (we call

7.1 The three
phases of a plosive

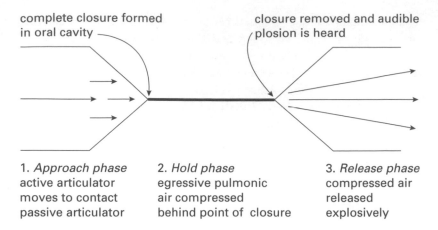

complete closure formed
in oral cavity

closure removed and audible
plosion is heard

1. *Approach phase*
active articulator
moves to contact
passive articulator

2. *Hold phase*
egressive pulmonic
air compressed
behind point of closure

3. *Release phase*
compressed air
released
explosively

this narrow approximation) we have a situation which is very familiar
to all of us because, as the air passes out from the lungs and through
this tiny narrow gap, the effect is going to be just like listening to the
wind hissing and whistling through a crack round a badly fitting door
or window, or like the steam forcing its way through the spout of a
kettle or between the lid and the rim of a pan of boiling water. It is
also rather like going for a bus ride! Late in the evening when there
are few people moving around, you can make nice smooth progress
onto the bus and find a seat without being bumped or jostled, but
try the same thing in the rush-hour and it's a very different scenario. You
move forward erratically, sometimes even move backwards, you are
pushed from one side and bump in turn into somebody else at the
other side, tempers flare and there is a lot of 'friction'! There are too
many people for the amount of space available. This emotional friction
is caused by your disturbed and irregular progress. It is directly analo-
gous to what happens to the lung air when it is forced through the
very small space left by the articulators. Instead of the big gap that is
created when you say a prolonged *aaah!*, for example, which is big
enough to let the air through in a nice smooth line without squashing,
jostling or disturbing it, the same amount of air is now required to get
through a very small space and so its progress is disturbed and the result

Fricative

is audible friction. Sounds produced in this way are called FRICATIVE.
So, when the lower lip rests lightly against the upper front teeth and
the air from the lungs is blown through between the two surfaces, forcing
a very tiny gap, we can hear friction being made at this labiodental place
of articulation. Like plosion, friction can occur on its own in voiceless
sounds or with the accompaniment of voice in voiced sounds. Hence,
in the English word *fever* we find first the voiceless labiodental fricative
[f] and then, between the two vowel sounds, the voiced labiodental
fricative [v].

EXERCISES

7.3 Add [f] and [v] to your list, together with their respective labels and a keyword for each. Can you discover any other fricatives in English? (There are nine altogether (including [f v].)

Which of these fricatives form voiceless/voiced pairs and which is the odd one out?

Add all nine fricatives to your list giving, in each case, the symbol, a keyword and the full VPM label.

In each case, think of six more English words that illustrate the sound.

7.4 1. Circle the words that begin and end with a fricative.

space	breath	hush	faith
loch	scratch	choose	tough
phase	this	rouge	though

2. Circle the words in which the fricative in the middle is voiced.

cosy	either	essay	ether
raisin	bristle	buzzing	buses
mother	cousin	easy	fishes

If we mix the two oral sound types that we have so far into a close-knit sequence of obstruction or stop followed by friction, we can come up with a third manner of articulation. Again we need to imagine an active articulator forming a firm closure against a passive articulator (as was the case for plosives). The air pressure builds up behind this obstruction, but this time, instead of separating the articulators to a fairly wide distance, we separate them just a little bit to form a very tiny gap, narrow median approximation instead of wide median approximation. This means that when the compressed air is released, it causes audible friction instead of a plosion. This is the effect we can hear in the middle of *itchy* and *edgy* and at the beginning and end of *church* and *judge*.

Sounds like these which we can define as a close-knit homorganic sequence of stop plus friction agreeing in voice, are termed AFFRICATE. **Affricate**

EXERCISES

7.5 Add these two affricates ([tʃ] and [dʒ]) to your English consonant list, taking care to give each the correct VPM labels and a suitable keyword.

Think of English words which give six more examples of each sound.

7.6 Given the definition of an affricate above – a close-knit homorganic sequence of stop + friction agreeing in voice – which of the following English words might be said to contain phonetic affricates?

fudge	cats	shop	joke
winch	cheque	fishing	watches
picture	champagne	leisure	refrigerator
words	mints	lethargy	sphinx

By comparison with these three new oral manners, vowels, as we have seen, are produced using a relatively unconstricted vocal tract. Some consonants are made this way too. The active articulator moves in the direction of the place of articulation, the passive articulator, but stops when it reaches a position of wide approximation. Vowel-like consonants **Approximant** of this kind are known collectively as APPROXIMANT consonants. English has four of these: [w j ɹ] and [l].

In articulatory terms, however, [l] is a little bit different from the other three. To find out how it differs, you will need to do a practical exercise.

EXERCISE

7.7 First say the nonsense syllable *wah* [wɑː] on an outward breath, just as you would normally speak. Then practise saying it making the first sound very long, [wwwɑː]. Then say it on an inward breath (just inhaling or sucking in air – don't worry about voicing or anything) still keeping the first sound as long as you can, and see where you can feel cold air.

Repeat this in turn with *jah* [jɑː] and then with *rah* [ɹɑː]. Each time concentrate on whereabouts in your mouth you feel cold air while repeating the syllable on an inward breath.

Finally, compare what you have felt for *wah*, *jah* and *rah* with *lah* [lɑː].

Comment

What you will probably have noticed if you managed this exercise is that you felt cold down the middle of your mouth for *wah, jah, rah,* but cold at the side, over the side(s) of your tongue, for *lah.* What this tells us is something about the airflow. For the first three, the air is passing along the mid-sagittal line and we can say there is median or CENTRAL airflow. But for [l], the air is obstructed in the middle by a firm closure between the tip of the tongue and the alveolar ridge and, instead, escapes across the SIDE RIM(S) of the tongue, held low and out of contact with the upper molars for this purpose. [w j ɹ] are therefore said to be median approximants while [l] is called a LATERAL approximant. In everyday usage, people tend to abbreviate these names, referring to the median group simply as 'approximant' and to the lateral group (there are other types of lateral approximant that we haven't encountered here) simply as 'lateral'. Approximants of all kinds are usually voiced.

Central

Side rim(s)

Lateral

EXERCISE

7.8 Using, Table 5.1 on p. 41, try to find the places of articulation for the four English approximant sounds and add them to your list of English consonants. Remember to include the symbol and a keyword. Your list should now be complete.

While it was a very good language for illustrating place of articulation, English is not quite so good for illustrating the range of manners of articulation that are found around the world. The five we have described above are less than half of the eleven or so different manners in use in world languages. However, English speakers often find that although they don't use them in any regular sense, they do make sounds with other manners of articulation from time to time. TRILL sounds and TAP sounds are two examples of these.

Trill

When learning to sing, or perhaps when declaiming Shakespeare in high rhetorical style, we are often encouraged to 'roll' the r-sounds. The effect of this is to produce a voiced alveolar trill. This is the normal way to pronounce 'r' in many languages. Many speakers of southern Dutch use it, for example, and it is heard in Spanish in a word like *perro* (dog) [pero]. You should note that this is the sound for which we write the phonetic symbol using the letter *r* the right way up! (Compare it with the usual British English [ɹ].)

Tap

The next manner may require you to do little bit of fieldwork if you want to hear people using the sound! A voiced alveolar tap, [ɾ] (like a single beat of the trill sequence) is used by many of us in certain words in our everyday English speech. Scottish speakers of English tend to use this variety when the sound occurs at the beginning of a word; South African speakers of English use it for all r-sounds; speakers of general Southern British English often use it as the r-sound in *three, through, thrifty* and older generations of speakers with this accent will be heard to say it in words like *very* and *worry* as well. Finally, it is the other type of r-sound used by speakers of Spanish, for example *pero* (but) [peɾo]. (Note the contrast here between the trill in *perro* and the tap in *pero* in Spanish.) Interestingly, speakers of English with an American accent also tend to use this sound, [ɾ], but for them it is a variety of the [t]-sound in the middle of words like *butter, better, water*.

Can you make these sounds yourself? Do you think you use either of them routinely in the way you speak English?

EXERCISE

7.9 Take a phrase like *red roses* or, better still, a sequence like the tongue-twister *Round the rugged rock the ragged rascal ran* and say it out loud, first using the voiced postalveolar approximant [ɹ] for all the r-sounds, then with the voiced alveolar trill and finally with the voiced alveolar tap. Get other people to say it for you – as many people as possible. What sort of r-sound do they use? And finally, if you can find a speaker of Spanish, ask them to make the difference between *perro* and *pero* for you and then try them out yourself and see if your Spanish friend can be certain which one you are saying.

A slightly different kind of articulatory gesture is used by many speakers of Dravidian languages in southern India for one of their r-sounds. For the alveolar tap, the tongue tip moves up and strikes once against the alveolar ridge, just like a single knock or tap at the door, for example. In the Dravidian sound, the tongue tip starts off curled up and back in what is called a retroflex position and then simply 'flaps' back down to the rest position, hitting the alveolar ridge on its way past! This sound, which has its own symbol [ɽ], is more of a relaxed flapping gesture than a deliberate tap and so it is given the manner label FLAP. It is the only sound of its manner recognized by the phonetic symbol chart of the International Phonetic Association: the voiced retroflex flap.

Flap

EXERCISE

7.10 Look carefully at the following passage of English.

1. Make lists of all the (a) plosives, (b) fricatives and (c) affricates you can find. Divide your lists into voiceless and voiced examples.

2. Excluding [ɹ], make a list of all the words that contain a median approximant.

> As they turned down the last lane of stalls, Milo noticed a wagon that seemed different from the rest. On its side was a small neatly lettered sign that said DO IT YOURSELF, and inside were twenty-six bins filled with all the letters of the alphabet from A to Z.
>
> 'These are for people who like to make their own words', the man in charge informed him. '[. . .] Here, taste an A; they're very good.'
>
> Milo nibbled carefully at the letter and discovered that it was quite sweet and delicious – just the way you'd expect an A to taste.
>
> 'I knew you'd like it', laughed the letter man, popping two Gs and an R into his mouth and letting the juice drip down his chin. 'A's are one of our most popular letters. All of them aren't so good', he confided in a low voice. 'Take the Z, for instance – very dry and sawdusty. . . . '
>
> (From *The Phantom Tollbooth* by Norton Juster)

SUMMARY

- In addition to nasals, ejectives, implosives and clicks, routine egressive pulmonic airflow through the oral cavity can be modified to produce plosives, fricatives, affricates, approximants, laterals, trills, a tap and a flap.

8

THE INTERNATIONAL PHONETIC ALPHABET

In this chapter, we will introduce the IPA chart and teach you to 'read' the entries through the development of your earlier work on voice, place and manner of articulation. (This will mean that even if you don't know what a particular sound actually sounds like, you will understand its location on the chart and something about how it is made.)

IPA CHART

IPA chart

Looking at the IPA CHART in Figure 8.1, you will see that there are a number of different sorts of information. There is the main grid (entitled 'CONSONANTS (PULMONIC)') containing only consonant sounds that are made using air from the lungs. Many of these will now be familiar to you because of the work done in earlier chapters of this book and because of your knowledge of English. Directly below on the left is a smaller grid containing symbols for sounds made using air other than air from the lungs, entitled 'CONSONANTS (NON-PULMONIC)'. These include sounds like the clicks (the 'kissing' sound, the 'tut-tut' sound, 'gcc-up', etc.). To the right of this box is a vowel diagram containing all the vowel symbols you have met so far and some more besides.

Consonants (pulmonic)

Consonants (non-pulmonic)

Immediately below the non-pulmonic consonants is a short list of 'OTHER SYMBOLS'. These are symbols which, for various reasons, won't fit into either of the two consonant grids. In most cases, these symbols represent double articulations (labial-velars, for example) which won't fit neatly into any one cell of the main grid; there is also a mechanism for coining new symbols to represent other double articulations and also affricates. This is the TIE BAR – a sort of diacritic (like an eyebrow over the top of two symbols), but different from other diacritics in the sense

Other symbols

Tie bar

that it creates a new sound rather than modifies and existing sound. Below these other symbols is a further grid containing the diacritics proper. As we have already seen, these are small symbols which can be applied to any of the main symbols (in the grids, etc.) in order to add further characteristics to the sound represented: [̥] removes the voicing from symbols representing voiced sounds (the chart illustrates a voiceless alveolar nasal, for example, of the sort you might hear in Burmese), [̪] is like a tiny picture of a tooth and can be applied to alveolar symbols to enable them to be used to represent dental sounds. Notice that in many cases, there is only one symbol or pair of symbols given for all the denti-alveolar places (dental, alveolar, postalveolar) – we use diacritics to move these backwards and forwards as required ([t̪] would be a voiceless dental plosive, [t] a voiceless alveolar on and [t̠] a voiceless postalveolar one); [̪] specifically makes the symbol represent a dental sound but if you wanted to make any other sound more forward in the mouth (ADVANCED is the technical term) you would have to put a little **Advanced** plus sign underneath as, for example, in this advanced voiceless velar plosive [k̟]. (You might encounter this articulation in an English word like *ski* [sk̟iː]; say *car key* slowly to yourself and try to feel the different points of contact between the tongue and the soft palate for the two [k]-sounds.) Another commonly used diacritic is one we have already discussed, [̃], which we said indicates the presence of simultaneous nasal airflow in a sound that is more often purely oral.

Finally, on the right of the page below the vowel diagram there is a list of symbols used for what are called 'SUPRASEGMENTALS'. These are **Suprasegmentals** features of spoken language that occur at the same time as, but in addition to, all the sound-based characteristics already discussed. [ː], for example, is the length mark which shows that the sound represented last for longer time rather than a shorter time. The stress mark that we mentioned earlier is also here [ˈ], as is a further application of the tie bar which can also be used to show that a speaker hasn't paused at a particular point, the speech runs on continuously. Symbols for marking tone and intonation are also listed here.

Clearly, even though not all the sounds are familiar, it is important to be able to find your way around in this information and to be able to 'read off' phonetic labels for particular symbols or to find the symbols that would be used for particular sound types. This is much more straightforward than it may at first appear, especially once you have mastered the axes of the main consonant grid. Along the horizontal axis are the places of articulation, arrayed exactly as you would find them, working from the lips inwards on a vocal tract drawing (lips on the left as you look at it, velum on the right). You could usefully correlate this with the list of places of articulation in Table 5.1 on p. 41 of this book.

CONSONANTS (PULMONIC)

	Bilabial	Labiodental	Dental	Alveolar	Postalveolar	Retroflex	Palatal	Velar	Uvular	Pharyngeal	Glottal
Plosive	p b			t d		ʈ ɖ	c ɟ	k ɡ	q ɢ		ʔ
Nasal	m	ɱ		n		ɳ	ɲ	ŋ	N		
Trill	ʙ			r					R		
Tap or Flap				ɾ		ɽ					
Fricative	ɸ β	f v	θ ð	s z	ʃ ʒ	ʂ ʐ	ç ʝ	x ɣ	χ ʁ	ħ ʕ	h ɦ
Lateral fricative				ɬ ɮ							
Approximant		ʋ		ɹ		ɻ	j	ɰ			
Lateral approximant				l		ɭ	ʎ	L			

Where symbols appear in pairs, the one to the right represents a voiced consonant. Shaded areas denote articulations judged impossible.

CONSONANTS (NON-PULMONIC)

Clicks		Voiced implosives		Ejectives	
ʘ	Bilabial	ɓ	Bilabial	ʼ	Examples:
ǀ	Dental	ɗ	Dental/alveolar	pʼ	Bilabial
ǃ	(Post)alveolar	ʄ	Palatal	tʼ	Dental/alveolar
ǂ	Palatoalveolar	ɠ	Velar	kʼ	Velar
ǁ	Alveolar lateral	ʛ	Uvular	sʼ	Alveolar fricative

VOWELS

Where symbols appear in pairs, the one to the right represents a rounded vowel.

OTHER SYMBOLS

ʍ Voiceless labial-velar fricative
w Voiced labial-velar approximant
ɥ Voiced labial-palatal approximant
ʜ Voiceless epiglottal fricative
ʢ Voiced epiglottal fricative
ʡ Epiglottal plosive

ɕ ʑ Alveolo-palatal fricatives
ɺ Alveolar lateral flap
ɧ Simultaneous ʃ and x

Affricates and double articulations can be represented by two symbols joined by a tie bar if necessary.

k͡p t͡s

DIACRITICS Diacritics may be placed above a symbol with a descender, e.g. ŋ̊

	Voiceless	n̥ d̥		Breathy voiced	b̤ a̤		Dental	t̪ d̪
	Voiced	s̬ t̬	~	Creaky voiced	b̰ a̰		Apical	t̺ d̺
ʰ	Aspirated	tʰ dʰ		Linguolabial	t̼ d̼		Laminal	t̻ d̻
	More rounded	ɔ̹	ʷ	Labialized	tʷ dʷ	~	Nasalized	ẽ
	Less rounded	ɔ̜	ʲ	Palatalized	tʲ dʲ	ⁿ	Nasal release	dⁿ
+	Advanced	u̟	ˠ	Velarized	tˠ dˠ	ˡ	Lateral release	dˡ
_	Retracted	e̠	ˤ	Pharyngealized	tˤ dˤ	̚	No audible release	d̚
¨	Centralized	ë	~	Velarized or pharyngealized	ɫ			
×	Mid-centralized	e̽	̝	Raised	e̝	(ɹ̝ = voiced alveolar fricative)		
	Syllabic	n̩	̞	Lowered	e̞	(β̞ = voiced bilabial approximant)		
	Non-syllabic	e̯	̘	Advanced Tongue Root	e̘			
~	Rhoticity	ɚ a˞	̙	Retracted Tongue Root	e̙			

SUPRASEGMENTALS

ˈ Primary stress
ˌ Secondary stress ˌfoʊnəˈtɪʃən
ː Long eː
ˑ Half-long eˑ
˘ Extra-short ĕ
| Minor (foot) group
‖ Major (intonation) group
. Syllable break ɹi.ækt
‿ Linking (absence of a break)

TONES AND WORD ACCENTS

LEVEL				CONTOUR		
e̋ or	˥	Extra high		ě or	˄	Rising
é	˦	High		ê	˅	Falling
ē	˧	Mid		e᷄	˧˦	High rising
è	˨	Low		e᷅		Low rising
ȅ	˩	Extra low		e᷈		Rising-falling
↓		Downstep		↗		Global rise
↑		Upstep		↘		Global fall

8.1 The International Phonetic Alphabet chart (revised to 1993, updated 1996). Reproduced by kind permission of the International Phonetic Association

EXERCISE

8.1 Look through the consonant symbols on the chart and find the place of articulation for each of the following sounds:

   1. [ɲ]   2. [q]   3. [ɴ]
   4. [ɸ]   5. [ɖ]   6. [z]
   7. [ʎ]   8. [ɾ]   9. [ɰ]
10. [χ]

(If a symbol is not in the main grid, you may have to look elsewhere on the chart to see if you are given any information that helps.)

In the main grid the vertical axis covers the manners of articulation for all sounds made with the egressive pulmonic airstream. The degree of stricture (space between the articulators) becomes gradually more open (from complete closure somewhere in the oral cavity for plosives and nasals at the top of the axis) through fricatives (narrow or close approximation) to approximants (wide or open approximation). Within the cells, where a pair of symbols is entered, the leftmost represents a voiceless version of the sound in question and the rightmost a voiced one. If you look at the row of entries for nasals, which are typically voiced sounds for most languages, you will find all the symbols on the right-hand side of the cells, in the 'voiced' position. If the ejectives, which are typically voiceless, were entered in such a grid, whereabouts in a cell would you expect to find the symbol? Yes, that's it, on the left-hand side of the cells, in the voiceless location.

If you look closely at the list of manners, you will notice that affricate is missing from the chart. Before you read on, can you figure out why this might be? In fact, it is because the chart contains all the information we need to make affricates for ourselves and so they do not need a separate entry: we have all the different plosive symbols (which constitute the first element of affricates) and all the different fricative symbols. All we need to do is to select the relevant two in any instance and join them together with the tie bar. So, if we want to symbolize a voiceless dental affricate we look first for the relevant plosive shape and find [t] covering the denti-alveolar positions and then, four rows below, we find the relevant fricative shape at the left-hand side of the dental fricative cell [θ]. If we write those next to each other and add a tie bar, we have the symbol for a voiceless dental affricate: [t͡θ].

EXERCISE

8.2 1. For each of the sounds in Exercise 8.1 above, check the line entry to determine the manner of articulation.

2. Sounds 2, 4, 6 and 10 could also be part of an affricate. Make up the appropriate symbol in each case and give the full voice–place–manner label for each resulting affricate sound.

3. What is the manner of articulation for [ʤ]?

VOWEL DESCRIPTION

Looking carefully at the vowel display on the IPA chart, you will find that wherever there is a pair of symbols, the right-hand one represents a rounded vowel. The labels front, central and back refer to the part of the tongue that is being used to make the vowel sound – you can infer from this that vowels are made between the palatal (front of tongue) and velar (back of tongue) articulatory positions. The vertical dimension, ranging from close, through CLOSE-MID, OPEN-MID to open, refers to how near to the passive articulator (the point along the roof of the mouth) the active articulator (the active part of the tongue) actually moves.

Close-mid
Open-mid

EXERCISE

8.3 One type of French has the sixteen-vowel system shown below. (Note that French schwa is rounded: [ɵ].)

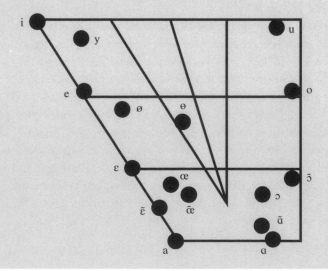

List the symbols for the following subsets of the French vowel system:

1. close vowels
2. close rounded vowels
3. back unrounded vowels
4. nasalized vowels
5. front rounded nasalized vowels

READING THE CHART

Supposing then (having started to familiarize yourself with the layout in the above exercises) you wished to use the chart to find the symbol representing a voiced uvular nasal: first find the row representing nasal consonants by looking down the vertical axis until you come to the label 'nasal'; then read along the place labels on the horizontal axis until you reach uvular. In the cell which represents the intersection of these two characteristics, you will find the symbol [ɴ] at the right-hand side – a voiced uvular nasal. Supposing you wanted to make this voiceless, say, or long, you would need to search for the appropriate diacritics to add to the basic symbol. Similarly, if you wanted a so-called double articulation (two places of articulation being used at the same time), a labial–uvular nasal for example, you would need to search for the bilabial nasal symbol and tie this (using the tie bar – the eye-brow above the two symbols) to the uvular symbol [m͡ɴ].

EXERCISES

8.4 Supply a phonetic symbol corresponding to each of the following labels:

1. voiceless dental fricative
2. voiceless alveolar nasal
3. voiced bilabial implosive
4. voiced palatalized alveolar lateral approximant
5. voiceless dental click
6. voiced labial–alveolar fricative
7. long back close rounded vowel
8. front open unrounded vowel
9. nasalized front close rounded vowel
10. back half-open (open mid) rounded vowel

8.5 Give full phonetic labels (voice–place–manner labels) for the sounds represented by the following symbols:

1. [n̺]
2. [ɢ]
3. [x]
4. [ɬ]
5. [ɹ̺]
6. [ɟ]
7. [ʋ]
8. [k͡ǁ]
9. [s']
10. [ç]

8.6 Pick any symbol from the grid at random and work out its full phonetic label until you feel confident that you know your way around in the cells.

Comment

Note that some cells in the grid are left empty. This is because although it is possible to make the sounds that would occur at such points, they have never been attested in any natural language – there has therefore never been a need for a symbol. Other cells are shaded. These indicate articulations which are thought to be physiologically impossible to make for various reasons. For example, you cannot make a voiced glottal plosive. The vocal folds cannot be held tightly closed (for the plosive) while simultaneously vibrating (for voice).

SUMMARY

•   The IPA chart contains all the basic tools needed to transcribe speech sounds: consonant symbols for primary or basic articulations in the main grid, additional symbols (which do not fit the grid, like double articulations), diacritics to modify all the basic symbols (vowels and consonants), vowel symbols, symbols for tone and intonation (which are beyond the scope of this workbook).

FURTHER EXERCISE

8.7 For each of the following, say whether or not they are possible articulations. If they are possible, suggest a suitable symbol. If they are impossible, explain briefly why.

1. voiced uvular lateral
2. ejective voiced velar plosive
3. labialized voiceless palatal fricative
4. voiceless pharyngeal nasal
5. nasalized long close front rounded vowel
6. voiceless alveolar retroflex fricative
7. nasalized devoiced velar approximant
8. back close open-mid rounded vowel
9. centralized front close-mid unrounded vowel
10. voiced bilabial lateral fricative approximant

9 MORE ABOUT CONSONANT VARIATION

This chapter introduces two phonetic features that are particularly associated with the production of obstruent consonants: aspiration and glottalization. As a function of aspiration, we will also introduce you to some new, non-English consonant sounds.

Obstruent

Sonorant

OBSTRUENT consonants are all those consonants which involve some kind of physical noise in their production: hissing or exploding, for example. As a collective term it can be used to refer to all plosives, fricatives and affricates. The antonym is SONORANT. This refers collectively to all sounds that give a resonant or sonorant sort of impression, like vowel sounds, with the complete absence of audible friction or plosion. Sonorants include nasals, laterals and approximant consonants (in addition to voiced vowels, of course).

EXERCISES

9.1 Excluding [h], make lists of all the obstruent consonants and all the sonorant consonants in English. Is there anything particular you notice about the obstruent groups?

9.2 Excluding [h], identify all the obstruents in the following data. Group them into voiced and voiceless.

That evening at my invitation a great friend of mine moved into the flat. The idea was that he should keep my spirits up. He was a man of gargantuan appetite and at midnight he produced a gargantuan meal of greasy chops served up with mounds of cabbage. It was a repast for which at any time I would have been unprepared [. . .] Tony finished my helping as well as his own.

'Must keep our strength up', he said [. . .]

At half past one in the morning I was finally woken by the telephone. 'Hallo', said a voice [. . .] 'Is that Mr Newby? It's me. Queen Charlotte's. It's all right, I'm happy to say. It's been born. Mrs Newby's comfortable. That means she's OK.'

'What's been born?'

'Half a mo. Let me check [. . .] It's a daughter. Is that what you wanted?'

'I don't mind as long as it's a baby. Thank you very much.'

[. . .] I woke Tony. Sitting up in bed we drank a bottle of champagne [. . .] and in the midst of more conventional toasts, we drank to Queen Charlotte's.

(From *Something Wholesale* by Eric Newby)

Look at your lists. What do you notice about the pronunciation of *s* suffixes (plural *s*, possessive *s*, verb endings, etc.) and about *ed*-suffixes?

What do you notice about the distribution of the sounds [θ] and [ð]?

What other observations can you make about obstruents in English on the basis of the data you have collected in these lists?

ASPIRATION is the name given to the h-like sound that is heard in many languages between the end of a voiceless consonant like a plosive, fricative or affricate, and the onset of vocal fold vibration for voicing in the vowel sounds that follows. This interval, while sounding like the exhalation of breath (an h-sound) is technically known as VOICE ONSET TIME (the time it takes between the end of the consonant in question and the onset of vocal fold vibration, voicing in the adjacent segment). Voice onset time is a slightly more general term than aspiration, because sometimes, when the sound that follows the consonant in question is another consonant rather than a vowel – an approximant, for example – there may still be this interval before the vocal folds start to vibrate. However, in such cases, we do not hear [h] but some other type of voiceless fricative sound which is related in articulatory terms to the approximant that is the eventual target.

Aspiration

Voice onset time

Compare the English words *pay* and *play* by saying them aloud to your-self a few times and listening carefully to the effect. (Although it is extremely widespread, not all English accents have aspiration. If you come from parts of Yorkshire, for example, this little experiment will not work for you and you will need to find a friend or teacher who speaks with a different accent – say a Southern British accent of some kind – to say the words for you.) For most speakers, then, you will hear a brief [h]-like interval between the [p] and the vowel in *pay* and a rather 'wet' or 'spitty' fricative-type of [l] in *play* (a sound like the so-called 'Welsh l' at the beginning of *Llandudno*, for example, [ɬ]). Effectively, in both cases, voicing is left out of the beginning of the following sound. We can show this in transcription by placing a zero-voicing diacritic below the symbol for the affected sound: [̥]. However, when the following sound is a vowel, because the auditory effect is perceived as [h] ([h], although we call it a voiceless glottal fricative, is actually any vowel made without vocal fold vibrations – a voiceless vowel) we tend to represent it using the aspiration diacritic, a raised small superscript [h]-symbol, [ʰ]. This would not be appropriate in contexts where a devoiced approximant consonant follows because in such cases, no h-sound is heard. Thus we begin to derive more detailed phonetic transcriptions. Instead of the broad phonetic transcriptions (or phonemic transcriptions) that we would have employed previously for our two test words, [peɪ] and [pleɪ] we can now note that these actually sound rather different from each other, [pʰeɪ] and [pl̥eɪ]. In the vast majority of English accents, aspiration is a crucial char-acteristic of all voiceless plosives when they occur initially in stressed syllables: *pie* [pʰaɪ], *tie* [tʰaɪ], *chi* [kʰaɪ], for example. (Note that after [s], the aspiration is lost – compare *pie* [pʰaɪ] and *spy* [spaɪ], where the [p] in *spy* will sound more like a [b], etc. – and is weak or non-existent at the beginning of unstressed syllables.)

In English, aspiration is an important characteristic of the sound of the language, but it does not have a linguistic function, it does not change the meaning. In other languages, Burmese and Korean for example, aspirated vs unaspirated is linguistically contrastive (that is, changes meaning like [p] and [b] can change meaning in English, or [p] and [s], giving *pin* vs *bin*, *pin* vs *sin*, etc.).

Voicing diagrams

We can use VOICING DIAGRAMS (another instance of parametric diagrams) to illustrate aspiration. Look at *pin* and *spin* (Figure 9.1 (a) and (b) respectively) and similarly, devoicing of approximant consonants as in *play* (Figure 9.1(c)). The zig-zag line represents voice and the flat line voicelessness.

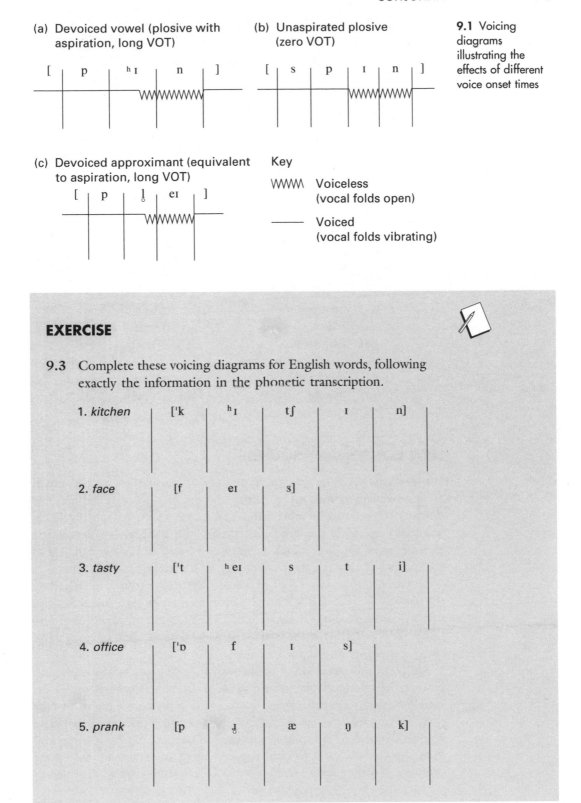

(a) Devoiced vowel (plosive with aspiration, long VOT)

[p ʰɪ n]

(b) Unaspirated plosive (zero VOT)

[s p ɪ n]

9.1 Voicing diagrams illustrating the effects of different voice onset times

(c) Devoiced approximant (equivalent to aspiration, long VOT)

[p l̥ eɪ]

Key

〰〰〰 Voiceless (vocal folds open)

───── Voiced (vocal folds vibrating)

EXERCISE

9.3 Complete these voicing diagrams for English words, following exactly the information in the phonetic transcription.

1. *kitchen*   ['k   ʰɪ   tʃ   ɪ   n]

2. *face*   [f   eɪ   s]

3. *tasty*   ['t   ʰeɪ   s   t   i]

4. *office*   ['ɒ   f   ɪ   s]

5. *prank*   [p   ɹ̥   æ   ŋ   k]

9.4 Draw voicing diagrams for the following words: *anything*, *father*, *splashing*, *stuffy*, *laughing*, *occur*, *remiss*, *skunk*, *sunflower*, *extravagant* (note stress position: *ex'travagant*).

9.5 Try reading the following Swahili data aloud. You will note that in the formation of the plural of these so-called u-class nouns, the initial obstruent of the plural form is aspirated while in the singular, in intervocalic position (i.e. between two vowels), it is not aspirated.

Note: to practise aspiration, hold a strip of tissue or other thin paper in front of your mouth and practise [pʰɑː] vs [pɑː] – when you aspirate the first of this pair, the paper will be displaced but it will stay relatively still for the second, the unaspirated version. (The unaspirated version needs to be rather more [b]-like.)

1. (a) [upamba]   'knife'   (b) [pʰamba]   'knives'
2. (a) [ukuta]   'wall'   (b) [kʰuta]   'walls'
3. (a) [utʃaŋgo]   'small   (b) [tʃʰaŋgo]   'small
                     intestine'   intestines'
4. (a) [utʃaguzi] 'election'   (b) [tʃʰaguzi] 'elections'
5. (a) [upepo]   'wind'   (b) [pʰepo]   'winds'

NEW CONSONANT SOUNDS

It is interesting to note that when the so-called 'aspiration process' affects an approximant consonant it causes the production of a phonetically different consonant altogether. Devoiced approximants are actually voiceless fricatives. [l̥] is therefore perceptually the same as [ɬ], a voiceless alveolar lateral fricative, which is the sound heard in Welsh, signalled in the spelling of that language by double-l: *Llangollen*, *Llanelli*, etc.

Similarly, the devoiced [w̥] in a word like *twin* [tw̥ɪn], is effectively the same as the voiceless labial–velar fricative used by speakers of English with a Scottish accent, for example, at the beginning of *wh*-words (*which* [ʍɪtʃ] as opposed to *witch* [wɪtʃ], or *why* [ʍaɪ] as opposed to *Υ/Wye* [waɪ], etc.). (See also Exercise 2.9.)

Although this has nothing to do with the operation of the aspiration process, the voiceless labial–velar fricative is also very closely related to the voiceless velar fricative that many speakers use at the end of the word *Loch* [lɒx] (as in *Loch Lomond* or the *Loch Ness monster)* instead of the more English k-sound. This sound is also used in German (where it is referred to as the *ach-laut*) and English speakers often use it at the end of the composer's name, *Bach* (again instead of a k-sound). The articulatory difference between labial–velar [ʍ] and velar [x] is that the former has lip rounding while the latter does not.

Devoicing [j] as in *pure, tune* or *cure* produces a sound known as a voiceless palatal fricative, symbolized [ç], which is also heard in the majority of accents of English at the beginning of words like *huge* and *humour* that we typically represent in our broad phonetic or phonemic transcription as [hj-]. This sound, [ç], is the German *ich-laut* as in *ich bin* ('I am') [ıç bın] or *München* (Munich) [mynçən]. (Try these sounds out for yourself.)

EXERCISES

9.6 Draw voicing diagrams for the following words and phrases.

    1. *München* (use German transcription above)
    2. *Llanelli* [ɬə'neɬi] (Anglicization of Welsh)
    3. [oluganda] (Ganda: 'the Ganda language')
    4. [nsqɛinm] (Squamish: 'rub oil in one's hair')
    5. [isitʰɔmbe] (Zulu: 'picture')
    6. [tʰunda] (Swahili: 'strings of beads')
    7. [ʔalk'uuk'] (Diryata: 'beans')
    8. [akʰostʰinniː] (Alabaman: 'think')
    9. [ŋkekere] (Efik: 'I was called')
    10. [lɘʋaɛŋ] (Cambodian: 'game')

9.7 Try reading the following data aloud. In each case, the vowels have been adapted where necessary.

    1. *Based on Welsh*

1.	[ɬɪn]	'lake'	2.	[ɬæːð]	'to kill'
3.	[ɬuːx]	'dust'	4.	[ɬaiθ]	'milk'
5.	['ɬænʊ]	'tide'	6.	[ɬæn]	'a church'
7.	['ɬɪneð]	'last year'	8.	[ɬau]	'hand'
9.	[gʊeɬ]	'better'	10.	['koːɬɪ]	'to miss'

    2. *Based on German*

1.	['ıç laʊt]	'ich-sound'	2.	['axlaʊt]	'ach-sound'
3.	['çıːna]	'China'	4.	[mɪlç]	'milk'
5.	[dax]	'roof'	6.	[kuːxən]	'cake'
7.	[eçt]	'real'	8.	[ɬɒx]	'hole'
9.	[fɔıçt]	'damp'	10.	[çı'miː]	'chemistry'

    3. *Based on Scottish English*
       (Remember to pronounce all the r-sounds here as well!)

1. Did you say [weər] or [ʍeər]?
2. [waɪ] and [ʍaɪ] are not the same!
3. I said [ʍɒt] not [wɒt].
4. [ʍɪtʃ wɪtʃ] played 'trick or treat'?
5. I wondered ['ʍeðər] the ['weðər] was fine?

Glottalization

GLOTTALIZATION, the concomitant articulation of a glottal stop along with some other articulation, is different again. Ejectives are sometimes classified as glottalized for this reason (remember the production mechanism for ejective consonants – see pp. 50–51). Alternatively, a glottal closure can be used to reinforce voicelessness in another consonant, as is often the case for (word-)final voiceless plosives in English. Possibly to ensure that no voicing creeps into these sounds at all from the preceding vowel or consonant, a glottal stop is often formed fractionally before the oral articulators establish the [p t k]-position. Once the oral **Glottalized** articulators are firmly in place, the glottis reopens, allowing the resump- **Preglottalized** tion of egressive pulmonic airflow. Such articulations are called **Glottal** GLOTTALIZED, or PREGLOTTALIZED or are said to be made with **reinforcement** GLOTTAL REINFORCEMENT. Such articulations are in free variation with realizations made without such glottalization: *hit* [hɪt] or [hɪʔt]. We can adapt voicing diagrams to produce parametric diagrams to illustrate this:

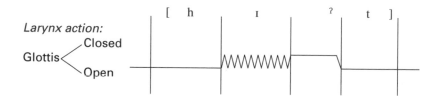

Larynx action:

Glottis — Closed / Open

Whether you do this or not in your own variety of English will depend again on your accent. Some accents completely replace final t-sounds with glottal stops anyway, and popular London ('Cockney') can replace all final voiceless plosives by the glottal stop, creating homophones *bap* (bread roll), *bat*, *back*, which can all be realized [bæʔ]. (See also Exercise 9.2 here.)

Typical environments for glottal reinforcement in many accents of British English are:

1. at the end of an utterance: either in isolation as in *art* [ɑːʔt], or as the first consonant of a cluster *arts* [ɑːʔts], *apt* [æʔpt];
2. at the end of a syllable when another consonant follows at the beginning of the next syllable: *art lesson* ['ɑːʔt 'lesn]. (Glottal

replacement of [t] in this environment is now also entirely acceptable in SBE.)

(The voiceless affricate [tʃ] can also undergo glottal reinforcement in the above environments and additionally, in intervocalic position (*archery* [ˈɑːʔtʃəɹi]).)

EXERCISE

9.8 Analyse the following data, listing separately words or phrases which could contain:

1. aspirated voiceless plosives (or the aspiration process)
2. unaspirated voiceless plosives
3. voiceless plosives which could have glottal reinforcement

Indicate the sound or sounds affected by either transcribing them or underlining. If there is more than one way of saying something, enter each alternative separately in your lists.

> The kitten was six weeks old. It was enchanting, a delicate fairy-tale cat, whose Siamese genes showed in the shape of the face, ears, tail, and the subtle lines of its body. Her back was tabby: from above or the back, she was a pretty tabby kitten, in grey and cream. But her front and stomach were a smoky-gold, Siamese, cream, with half-bars of black at the neck. Her face was pencilled with black – fine dark rings around the eyes, fine dark streaks on her cheeks, a tiny cream-coloured nose with a pink tip, outlined in black. From the front, sitting with her slender paws straight, she was an exotically beautiful beast. She sat, a tiny thing, in the middle of a yellow carpet, surrounded by five worshippers, not at all afraid of us. Then she stalked around that floor of the house, inspecting every inch of it, climbed up to my bed, crept under the fold of a sheet, and was at home.
>
> (From *Particularly Cats* by Doris Lessing)

Is there any possibility of a [tʃ] with glottal reinforcement in these data?

SUMMARY

- Plosives, fricatives and affricates can be referred to collectively as obstruents.
- Additional consonantal variation can be obtained by aspirating and/or glottalizing obstruents.
- Aspiration is essentially a delay in the onset of vocal fold vibration in a following voiced sound after completion of an obstruent articulation; this measurable interval of voicelessness is called voice onset time.

YET MORE ABOUT CONSONANTS: SECONDARY ARTICULATIONS

10

In this final chapter, we will introduce the concepts of double articulation (briefly mentioned in Chapter 5) and secondary articulation (labialization, palatalization and velarization) together with the relevant notational diacritics. This will introduce you to the remaining segmental materials on the IPA chart.

DOUBLE ARTICULATION

Like diacritics (which we add to other basic sound symbols to modify them in some way) the symbols for double articulations cannot be found in the main grid of the phonetic alphabet chart. This is because each box in the grid correlates with one place of articulation only and a double articulation, as its name suggests, involves two articulations at the same time and, therefore, two separate places of articulation. If you want to represent such sounds on a grid then you either have to enter them twice, once at each place (which is not really satisfactory because it implies that they are two different things) or create special 'double-place' boxes in the grid for them. The only other alternative is to list them separately. The present edition of the IPA chart chooses to do the latter. Symbols for double articulations can be found entered under the list of 'OTHER SYMBOLS', bottom left below the main grid.

To be classified as a double articulation, a sound must be produced with two simultaneous articulations of equal stricture which (obviously, because they are simultaneous) also agree in voice. For example, you might find two gestures both of wide approximation such as we have in the English voiced labial–velar approximant [w]; two gestures of narrow approximation, such as the voiceless labial–velar fricative that we have just discussed above, [ʍ]; or two gestures of complete closure such as you hear people doing when they are trying to imitate chickens clucking and they make a k-sound and a p-sound at the same time, a voiceless labial–velar plosive [k͡p]. This last sound can also be made voiced and the two sounds [k͡p] and [g͡b] are found in many African languages, especially those spoken in Nigeria such as Igbo, Kpelle, Ga, etc.

English has other consonants which, phonetically, can be classified as double articulations. The English [ɹ]-sound, for example, has open postalveolar approximation. Simultaneously, however, it has open lip rounding (not at all unlike [w]). Technically, therefore, we are dealing with a *labial*–postalveolar approximant. Likewise palatoalveolar [ʃ] and [ʒ] (called, misleadingly, postalveolar by the IPA) have simultaneous narrow approximation at the palate and the alveolar ridge.

Another double articulation, familiar to all speakers and learners of French, is the labial–palatal [ɥ] found as the second consonant in words like *lui* (to him) [lɥi], *juin* (June) [ʒɥɛ̃], *juillet* (July) [ʒɥije].

EXERCISE

10.1 The following are all potential double articulations. Use the IPA chart on p. 66 to work out the full VPM labels in each case.

1. [pt]   2. [ɸç]   3. [zv]
4. [bɢ]   5. [mn]   6. [gd]
7. [ʋj]   8. [ʃf]   9. [rʀ]
10. [βɣ]

Can you make up any more double articulations?

Note that if you want to make quite sure that what you write is interpreted by the reader as a double articulation and not as a sequence of two discrete sounds, you can join the symbols using a tie bar (see 'Other symbols' on the phonetic alphabet chart): [k͡p], [m͡n], etc.

EXERCISES

10.2 Indicate which of the following could be double articulations and which are just single articulations or sequences of two separate consonant sounds.

1. [gb]   2. [sf]   3. [pɸ]
4. [nl]   5. [mŋ]   6. [g☉]
7. [ɥ]   8. [ɰ]   9. [tʃ]
10. [kj]

10.3 All clicks are double articulations. Can you say why? (You might need to look again at the account of click production on p. 54.)

10.4 Why might rounded vowels be considered double articulations?

SECONDARY ARTICULATION

Many languages use articulatory gestures known as SECONDARY ARTIC-ULATIONS to create differences in consonant sounds over and above those provided for by the range of single and double articulations that we have looked at so far. As the name suggests, the presence of a secondary articulation in the production of a speech sound implies that although there are again two things happening at the same time they are somehow of different importance, one of them is primary while the other is secondary – one ranks higher, in some way, than the other. Ranking of gestures is based on the degree of approximation between the artic-ulators, the width of the stricture between the active and passive articulators: the narrower the gap, the higher the gesture ranks. So, complete closure (as in the production of plosives, for example) ranks higher than anything, while open approximation (of the type used to produce approximants and vowels) ranks bottom. This can give us a rough three-rank scale:

1. plosive
2. fricative
3. approximant, vowel

Fortunately, the range of places at which secondary articulations typically occur is by no means as extensive as the range for primary (i.e. single) articulations (see p. 40). Secondary articulations seem to occur at the bilabial, palatal, velar or pharyngeal positions only.

Thus, if you take a word like English *tea* [tiː] and compare it (looking in the mirror, preferably) with English *too/two* [tuː], you will notice that the lip position differs during the production of the t-sound. It is unrounded in tea but rounded in *two* (see Fig. 10.1). We say that the t-sound in *too/two* has undergone LABIALIZATION, that it is LABIAL-IZED. We can transcribe this difference with the help of the lip rounding

Secondary articulation

Labialization
Labialized

Coarticulation

or labialization diacritic: [tiː] vs [tʷuː]. In English, labialization is a form of assimilation – the COARTICULATION of a mix of articulatory gestures from adjacent sounds, the lips are anticipating, assimilating to, the rounded position required for the next sound.

10.1 Lip positions during the articulation of English [t]

The lips during the [t] in *tea*   The lips during the [t] in *two*

Labialization can, however, be a deliberate gesture, designed to make a contrast between two sounds, [k] vs [kʷ] say. Many languages have a series of plain consonants, primary articulations by themselves, in contrast with a series of labialized ones: Amharic, Ubyx and Gilbertese, for example.

EXERCISES

10.5 All English consonants (except those that already have lip rounding: [w ʃ ʒ ɹ]) will be labialized in the environment of an immediately following rounded sound, either another consonant with lip rounding or a rounded vowel. Go through the following data and note, in transcribed form, all such *labialized* consonants.

> He often seemed to sit, absolutely immobile, for fifteen hours at a stretch [. . .] I would sometimes see him in the morning, silhouetted against a frosted-glass door, with his right hand apparently motionless a few inches from his knee. I might catch sight of him later [. . .] with his hand 'frozen' halfway to his nose [. . .] Then a couple of hours later, his hand would be frozen on his glasses or his nose [. . .] It was only much later, when he was awakened [. . .] that the incredible truth came out [. . .]
> 'What do you mean "frozen poses"?' he exclaimed. 'I was merely wiping my nose!'
> 'But Miron, this just isn't possible. Are you telling me that what I saw as frozen poses was your hand in transit to your nose? [. . .] Do you mean to tell me that you were taking six hours to wipe your nose?'

'It sounds crazy', he reflected, 'and scary, too. To me they were just normal movements, they took a second. You want to tell me I was taking hours instead of seconds to wipe my nose?'
I didn't know what to answer. I was as nonplussed as he [. . .] Now, incredibly, I saw that the 'impossible' was true; using what amounted to time-lapse photography, I saw that the succession of 'poses' did, in fact, form a continuous action. He was, indeed, just wiping his nose, *but doing so ten thousand times slower than normal*.

(From *Awakenings* by Oliver Sacks)

10.6 Gilbertese has the following consonant system. Give full VPM labels for each of the sounds.

				t	k		kʷ
b		bʷ					
m	mː	mʷ	mːʷ	n	ŋ	ŋː	
			r				

The remaining secondary articulations all add a specific vowel resonance to the consonants. For example, close front vowels are made with the front of the tongue raised in open approximation to the hard palate. If this gesture is combined with another articulatory gesture, bilabial closure for example in [p] or [b], it adds an [i]-type resonance, giving [pʲ] and [bʲ] respectively (see palatalized [lʲ] in Fig. 10.2). The sounds undergo PALATALIZATION. They are said to be PALATALIZED. Such sounds are heard in English, especially in [j]-pronouncing accents in words like *pure* [pʲjʊə], *beauty* [bʲjuːti], *new* [nʲjuː], etc. Again, languages operate this characteristic contrastively as in Russian, Bulgarian and Kitja.

Palatalization
Palatalized

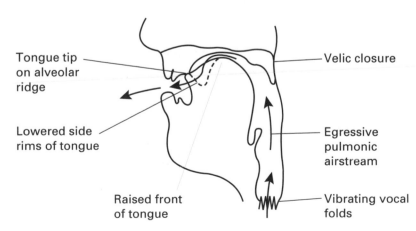

Tongue tip on alveolar ridge

Lowered side rims of tongue

Raised front of tongue

Velic closure

Egressive pulmonic airstream

Vibrating vocal folds

10.2 The front of the tongue raised during the production of [lʲ]

Velarization
Velarized

Back-tongue raising in open approximation to the velum adds a close back vowel resonance of an [ɯ]-type ([u] but without the lip rounding). The process is known as VELARIZATION and sounds affected are said to be VELARIZED. The IPA offers two different notations for velarization. The preferred notation for our present purposes is the addition of a tilde through the centre of the symbol, giving for example [ɫ], the velarized voiced alveolar lateral approximant.

The difference between palatalization and velarization can be heard in the pronunciation of the l-sound in the vast majority of English accents. Irish Gaelic also has these two types of l-sounds: saying *good-bye for now* to someone, *Slán go fóill*, you will find a velarized [l] in the first word [sɫɑːn] and a palatalized one in the last [foːlʲ]. If you have an English accent from the extreme northwest of England, however, or from Scotland or if you are a speaker of American English, then you will only have one of the variants, usually the velarized one, but most other speakers of English will find that they have a palatalized voiced alveolar lateral before a vowel (try *look, let, like, below, allow, falling*, etc., listening carefully and perhaps making the l-sound last a bit longer than usual) and a velarized one at the ends of words or before a consonant (try *ill, all, well, film, milk* and possibly also *middle, kettle*, etc., again listening carefully and prolonging the [ɫ]-sound a bit if you can).

The impressionistic names which you will find in many books for these two l-sounds are *clear-l* (for the palatalized one) and *dark-l* (for the velarized). In one or two accents of English, dark-l is pronounced as a vowel sound and so the only l-sound speakers of these accents use is the palatalized one that occurs before vowels. Speakers with a popular London accent, for example, will pronounce words such as *well, film, middle* as [weo, fɪom, mɪdo], with no l-sound at all.

Although in English these differences merely mark a difference of pronunciation or accent, some languages use palatalization and velarization

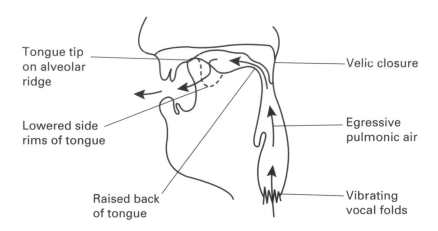

Tongue tip on alveolar ridge

Velic closure

Lowered side rims of tongue

Egressive pulmonic air

10.3 The back of the tongue raised during the production of [ɫ]

Raised back of tongue

Vibrating vocal folds

contrastively and some languages, Russian for example, use these two secondary articulations contrasting with each other. With the exception of the velars [k g x], Russian has no 'plain' consonants (that is, consonants without a secondary articulation), but two series in contrast with each other, one palatalized and the other velarized. The impressionistic names for these are *soft* and *hard* consonants respectively. Romany, Polish and Lithuanian use palatalized in contrast with plain and Kurdish makes very limited use of velarized in contrast with plain.

EXERCISES

10.7 Study the following data carefully and compile two separate lists, one containing all examples of palatalized laterals and the other velarized laterals. (Note that it doesn't really matter whether you pronounce dark-l or not in your own accent – you can still know about its use and distribution in other people's speech.) Further, indicate which, if any, would undergo devoicing as a function of the aspiration process.

> I hauled Gosfield Maid round in a shamble of flapping sails and gave way to the Isle of Wight, which steamed briskly off to starboard. This was not how I had planned things. My idea, sketched out long ago, had been that I would pilot my parents across the lonely face of the sea in a neat reversal of roles; the son would turn father, with all a father's air of calm and baffling expertise in the world.
>
> The trouble was, I didn't know the ropes. Learning to manage the boat single-handed, I hadn't bothered to take in their names. In any case, I was vain about not going in for the sort of salty talk which the amateur sailors like to sprinkle over their prose in Yachting Monthly and their conversation in yacht club bars. Let them keep their vangs and kicking-straps and halyards – I meant to live in ordinary daily English. What I hadn't reckoned on was that this made me perfectly unable to communicate the simplest instruction to my anxious-to-help father, who had done a bit of sailing in his time.
>
> 'Not that rope. The other one. The one next to it – the one that's tied to that cleat thing.'
>
> 'The topping lift', my father said, producing a surprise trump.
>
> (From *Coasting* by Jonathan Raban)

10.8 Now do the same for the passage in Exercise 10.5 above and/or for other passages of your own choice.

**Pharyngealiza-
tion**

Pharyngealized

(PHARYNGEALIZATION, the addition of an open back vowel resonance of the [ɑ]-type to consonants, will not be considered in detail here but it is used to make the so-called *emphatic* consonants – another impressionistic name – in nearly all varieties of Arabic and is heard for example in the l-sound in the name of God, *Allah*. Sounds modified in this way are said to be PHARYNGEALIZED.)

SUMMARY

- Strictures can be ranked according to the degree of approximation (the distance between the active and passive articulators) with complete closure ranking highest and open approximation lowest.
- When two articulations occur simultaneously, they can be accorded primary, secondary or equal status by looking at how the strictures involved rank: if they are equal, the sound is a double articulation, if one ranks higher than the other, the highest ranking is called the primary articulation while the lower one becomes the secondary articulation.

APPENDIX: WORKING WITH PHONETICS

One of the questions I am frequently asked by students enjoying studying this subject is: *Are there any jobs where I can use phonetics?* The answer is that there are all sorts of jobs where knowledge of phonetics is an advantage and some where it is an absolute requirement. This appendix looks briefly at a few of these jobs and what they might entail.

Phonetics is used by all sorts of people. It is used in at least two of the professions allied to medicine, speech therapy and audiology. In education, phonetics is not just a subject of study in its own right, but it is also an important tool in language teaching and learning (English as well as any other modern languages), drama studies, singing and so on; it even features in many UK secondary school English Language syllabuses. Phonetics interfaces with the law both in forensic phonetics and in other less obvious areas like issues over product names and trademarks. Phonetics is important in the theatre and the media (accent coaching and voice production, for example, rely on phonetic knowledge). Publishers rely on phonetics for dictionaries, foreign language courses and travellers' phrase books. Knowledge of phonetics is also immensely important in the technological revolution, both in voice activated systems (security devices, telephone banking systems, etc.) and also devices that 'speak' (from toys to talking computers). I could go on but this is perhaps enough to give you some idea of what phoneticians can do beyond the teaching of phonetics as an academic subject. Let's have a closer look at one or two of these applications.

In the field of SPEECH THERAPY, speech and language therapists spend their time helping people with communication disorders. Sometimes these are children who are having difficulty in acquiring speech and making themselves understood, sometimes adults who have lost all or part of their capacity for speech because of illness, accident or trauma of some kind. We've already met one therapy-related condition in this book. In Chapter 6, you read about a speaker who was unable to produce nasal consonants – the sort of thing that happens to us when we have a bad

Speech therapy

Hyponasality

cold and our nose is blocked. This effect can be described as HYPONASAL-ITY. It is quite the opposite of the problem that some people experience where their velum may be weak and won't stay closed and a plosive sound, for example, will start off OK but then turn into a homorganic nasal – *tuba* ['tjuːbə] may turn into something like ['tnj̃ũːbm̃ə] for example, or *daddy* ['dædi] into ['dnæ̃dnĩ]. Here, the speaker has too much nasal air-flow rather than too little. The most extreme cases of this kind are when a person has a cleft-palate where air escapes continuously into the nasal cavities while they are speaking via a gap in the palate in the roof of the mouth. This effect is described as HYPERNASALITY.

Hypernasality

Both speech therapy and audiology can be studied at degree level in UK universities. Speech therapy degrees have long been established; audiology degrees are newer and the degree-level training programme still less well established than in the US, for example. In both disciplines, there are pro-visions for graduate entry and in both phonetics will feature on the cur-riculum. There are several books that will start to give you more insight into these professions including *Linguistics in Clinical Practice* (1995, edited by Kim Grundy and published by Whurr Publishers, London), *Phonetics for Speech Pathology* (1993, 2nd edition, by Martin Ball and published by Whurr Publishers, London) and *Careers in Audiology* pub-lished by the British Society of Audiology (1998, 3rd edition). Further information is also available at the websites of the Royal College of Speech and Language Therapy (at http://www.rcslt.org.uk) and the British Society of Audiology (at http://www.b-s-a.demon.co.uk). Finally, *A Career in Speech and Language Therapy* (2005, by Janet Wright and Myra Kersner and published by Metacom Education, London) offers a truly comprehensive introduction to this worthwhile career.

Forensic phonetics

To work in FORENSIC PHONETICS, you need a good grasp of articu-latory phonetics and excellent ears (just like speech therapists, in fact) and also advanced expertise in acoustic phonetics (the physics of speech). Degrees or diplomas in forensic phonetics don't exist. You will have trained, either as an undergraduate or postgraduate, on a degree pro-gramme that hones your basic phonetic skills to quite a high level, and then you will need, effectively, an 'apprenticeship' – forging links with existing practitioners and working your way into the field through care-fully mentored training on the job. The work can be unpredictable, gru-elling, nerve-wracking, exciting and challenging! There are very few full-time openings in this field.

Forensic phoneticians need to be able to make very accurate auditory analyses of all sorts of different accents, making transcriptions (usually orthographic, for courtroom use, but phonetic for their own analytical purposes) of recorded materials. Phonetically, they need to be able to spot identifying characteristics or patterns in people's speech. They also need to be able to spot inconsistencies which tend to occur when a speaker is trying to disguise their accent or voice to avoid being recognized. They need to be able to identify and analyse differences in the acoustic images of speech (we call these SPEECH SPECTROGRAMS) and authenticate tape recordings (has the tape been tampered with? is it genuine?) and here again spectrographic analysis is often important. Moreover, they need to be able to do all this working with what are often very poor quality recordings. These recordings are often obtained from telephone conversations (and the telephone itself limits the amount of useful information the recording will contain) and they are often quite short (criminals, it seems, dislike holding long conversations).

Speech spectrograms

If you are interested in finding out more about acoustic phonetics, you can download a free speech analysis programme like 'Wasp' (available from http://www.phon.ucl.ac.uk/resource/sfs/wasp.htm) or 'Praat' (which means 'talk' in Dutch and is available from http://www.fon.hum. uva.nl/praat/). Make spectrograms of short utterances and try to analyse the images that result. (*Tip*: keep it simple and be systematic – start with short words like *bye, bay, boy, beer, bough* . . . *pie, pay* . . . *shy* . . . only changing one segment at a time until you start to get used to what you are looking at.)

For more information about the forensic applications of phonetics, you might like to look at books such as Phil Rose's *Forensic Speaker Identification* (2002, Taylor & Francis, London), Harry Hollien's *The Acoustics of Crime: the New Science of Forensic Phonetics* (1990, Plenum, New York) or Francis Nolan's *The Phonetic Bases of Speaker Recognition* (1983, Cambridge University Press, Cambridge). You might also like to browse in volumes of the *Journal of Forensic Linguistics*.

Many of the other areas of phonetic application (theatre, media, publishing) all have a certain amount in common. They share the need to communicate facts about pronunciation to a wide range of people, many of whom will have no formal phonetic knowledge at all. In many cases, they try to resolve this difficulty by coming up with some form of so-called PHONETIC SPELLING that will enable them to transmit details about pronunciation without the recipient being able to read transcription. Take a sound like Dutch [χ], for example: English does not have a sound like this voiceless uvular fricative, but many speakers of English use another very similar 'guttural' sound, [x], at the end of words like Scottish *loch*. A phonetic spelling for this sound is often 'ch'. Problems of this kind occur when compiling pronunciation guides for travellers or writing language textbooks or advising newsreaders, programme presenters and other speakers in the media services. To learn more about the work of the specialist team employed in the BBC's Pronunciation Unit, you might like to read an article by the previous Head, Graham Pointon, called 'The BBC and English Pronunciation' which you can find in the journal *English Today* (1988, vol. 15: 8–12).

Phonetic spelling

Voice coaching
Accent coaching

In the theatre, the most frequent applications of phonetic knowledge are VOICE COACHING and ACCENT COACHING. While the former requires an intimate knowledge of the breathing mechanism and posture, a good knowledge of articulatory phonetics will also be helpful; there is an overlap here, too, with the work of the speech therapist who also deals with remediation of voice disorders some of which will be the direct result of incorrect breathing and sound projection which often place a great strain on the vocal folds and the larynx.

Accent coaching, by contrast, requires expertise in articulatory phonetics and considerable skill in auditory phonetics – hearing and identifying and describing exactly which sounds and sound patterns are required and then monitoring and correcting the learner's output. It is the job of the accent coach to enhance the ability for mimicry that lies in all of us (more hidden in some than in others). Don't forget, you speak largely what you hear. A young person or child who is born in South Wales and starts his or her speaking life with a South Wales accent will, on moving to Newcastle, very quickly adapt to the local speech patterns and may, indeed, lose their original accent altogether. The more 'elderly' parents (in speech terms) are much less likely to effect this change – they have largely stopped listening, they no longer feel it imperative to 'fit in' with peer groups, they have already established their identities and self-image and may even be making a conscious social or political statement through retention of their original accent. Children who move around the country a lot while they are young, often end up with very hybrid accents as adults so that it is difficult to place exactly where they come from but possible to trace a number of apparently unconnected features in their accent. Anyway, the accent coach will try to recapture the child's ear for sound and the body's ability to translate what is heard into speech.

There are many ways in which this can be done, but one of the best is totally centred on 'ear-training'. A 'native-speaker' of an accent records a specially constructed passage which contains all the salient features of the accent (a book full of such passages is *The Voice Book* by Michael McCallion, the revised edition published in 1998 by Routledge, London). The learner (the actor or actress) will then listen to this tape over and over again, picking up details and imitating them as closely as possible before trying to extend their repertoire, as it were, and start to use the features on other pieces of text and eventually work with the script for the accented role they need to play in the drama in question.

So, these are some of the ways in which you can use your phonetic interest and skills in the workplace. There are many more, including opportunities for fieldwork (often through related disciplines such as linguistics, sociolinguistics and anthropology) and teaching and researching in the discipline itself. If you are really interested in taking things further you might consider entering for the International Phonetic Association's examination leading to the Certificate of Proficiency in the Phonetics of English. For full information about this examination (the syllabus, specimen questions, application form, fee, etc.) you can visit http://www. phon.ucl.ac.uk/home/wells/ipa-exam.htm either directly or via the IPA homepage (address below). You might also consider becoming a (student) member of the IPA and/or subscribing to a (free) electronic newsletter such as *foNETiks*. For information about these and about the International Phonetic Association in general, visit: http://www2.arts. gla.ac.uk/ipa.html

FURTHER READING

If you want to read more widely around the subject matter introduced in this book, we recommend the following:

General phonetics
Ladefoged, P. (2001, 4th edition) *Course in Phonetics*. Fort Worth, Harcourt Brace College Publishers.
This remains one of the leading textbooks on the market at the moment for the beginner and includes information on the physics of speech.

O'Connor, J. D. (1980, 2nd edition) *Phonetics*. Cambridge: CUP.
This introduction to general phonetics still makes for instructional reading that is enjoyed by many students. It is more traditional in approach and presentation than Ladefoged 2001 (see above).

English phonetics
Collins, B. and Mees, I. (2003) *Practical Phonetics and Phonology*. London: Routledge.
Correctly described as a 'resource book for students' this new textbook provides lots of easy-to-read information about the phonetics and phonology of English – good, clear diagrams, exercises (with access to on-line answers), a CD full of accent data plus a selection of pronunciation-related readings from books by other established authors.

Cruttenden, A. (ed.) (2001, 6th edition) *Gimson's Pronunciation of English*. London: Edward Arnold.
The sixth edition of this seminal reference text for English phonetics is a unique publication and a must for all serious and more advanced students of English phonetics.

Roach, P. J. (2001, 3rd edition) *English Phonetics and Phonology. A Practical Course*. Cambridge: CUP.

This book continues to be enjoyed by many students and comes with useful audio tapes/CDs. It is much simpler and less detailed than Cruttenden 2001.

Trudgill, P. (1994) *Dialects*. London: Routledge.
A further volume in this Language Workbook series, *Dialects* offers the reader further, less technically phonetic insight into dialect and accent variation.

Dictionaries
Wells, J. C. (2000) *Longman Pronunciation Dictionary*. London: Longman.
This dictionary is an invaluable asset for any student of general and/or English phonetics. It is not only one of the most comprehensive and up-to-date pronouncing dictionaries (offering comparative information on British and General American pronunciation) but also a mine of theoretical phonetic information with explanatory and well-illustrated gobbets under all salient headwords (aspiration, stress, weak vowel, etc.). If you are only going to invest in one other volume for your phonetics library, then this is the one I would recommend.

Trask, L. (1996) *Dictionary of Phonetics and Phonology*. London: Routledge.
Not a pronouncing dictionary, but an extended glossary of technical terms currently used in phonetic and phonological theory. A useful reference book.

Practical phonetics
Wells, J. C. and Colson, G. (1971) *Practical Phonetics*. Bath: Pitman Press.
The popularity and value of this little volume does not diminish.

Phonetics and the pronunciation of English
For the many non-native speakers of English whose primary purpose in learning phonetics is to improve and develop pronunciation skills (either as teachers or learners), the following phonetically motivated volumes can be recommended:

Gimson, A. C. (1975) *A Practical Course of English Pronunciation: A Perceptual Approach*. London: Arnold.
This volume with accompanying recorded materials includes excellent 'ear-training' exercises for the discrimination of English vowels, consonants and tonal patterns from each other and from non-English sounds.

O'Connor, J. D. and Fletcher, C. (1989) *Sounds English*. London: Longman.

The authors assist you in determining which exercises will be most beneficial by identifying typical problems encountered by learners of English for a wide variety of different first languages/mother tongues.

For those who want to take their study of phonetics further and read more widely but still not at a truly advanced level, I recommend the following texts:

Intonation
Cruttenden, A. (2000) *Intonation*. Cambridge: CUP.
There is very little available on English intonation by way of textbooks at the moment. One of the more reliable volumes (although still with some inconsistencies) is this one by Allan Cruttenden.

English accents
Hughes, A. and Trudgill, P. (1987, 2nd edition) *English Accents and Dialects*. London: Edward Arnold.
This volume benefits from recordings of a number of different regional accents.

Wells, J. C. (1982) *Accents of English*. Vols 1-3. Cambridge: CUP.
An excellent comparative study of English pronunciation worldwide, but difficult volumes for the beginner.

Physics of speech
Ball, M. J. and Rahilly, J. (1999) *Phonetics. The Science of Speech*. London: Arnold.
A couple of useful chapters on the acoustics and perception of speech plus another on instrumental phonetics conclude this volume.

Borden, Gloria J., Harris, Katherine S. and Lawrence, J. Raphael (1994, 3rd edition) *Speech Science Primer: Physiology, Acoustics and Perception of Speech*. Baltimore: Williams & Wilkins.
A lavishly illustrated and detailed account of the subject which sets the (acoustic) study of speech against a wider backdrop of speech, language and thought.

Brosnahan, L. and Malmberg, Bertil (1970) *Introduction to Phonetics*. Cambridge: CUP.
Denes, Peter B. and Pinson, E. (1993, 2nd edition) *The Speech Chain – The Physics and Biology of Spoken Languages*. New York: Anchor Books.
Fry, D. (1979) *The Physics of Speech*. Cambridge: CUP.
These three easy-to-read volumes provide clear introductions to acoustic phonetics but with less in-depth coverage of the articulatory phonetic interface than any of the other volumes recommended in this section.

Johnson, Keith (2003, 2nd edition) *Acoustic and Auditory Phonetics.* Oxford: Blackwell.
A more advanced and detailed account of acoustic phonetics and speech perception.

Phonetic representation of speech sounds
(1999) *Handbook of the International Phonetic Association: A Guide to the Use of the International Phonetic Alphabet*, Cambridge: CUP.
The professional handbook and guide to the IPA and its alphabet. Used by phoneticians the world over, this volume includes valuable illustrations of the application of the IPA to the phonetic description of languages. Interactive CD Rom available.

Pullum, G. K. and Ladusaw, W. (1986) *Phonetic Symbol Guide.* Chicago: The University of Chicago Press.
A clear, interesting and informative volume on symbol shapes and names.

Finally, all of the following volumes are advanced, up-to-date publications which will take you forward in the core areas of articulatory, auditory and acoustic phonetics to a level well beyond that covered in many volumes mentioned earlier in this list:

Advanced general phonetics
Hardcastle, William J. and Laver, John (eds) (1997) *The Handbook of Phonetic Sciences.* Oxford: Blackwell.
Ladefoged, P. (2005, 2nd edition) *Vowels and Consonants. An Introduction to the Sounds of Language.* Oxford: Blackwell.
Ladefoged, P. and Maddieson, Ian (1996) *Sounds of the World's Languages.* Oxford: Blackwell.
Laver, J. (1994) *Principles of Phonetics.* Cambridge: CUP.

Experimental phonetics
Hayward, Katrina (2000) *Experimental Phonetics.* Harlow: Longman.
Lass, N. (ed.) (1996) *Principles of Experimental Phonetics.* St Louis, MI: Mosby.

ANSWERS TO EXERCISES

UNIT 1   SPOKEN AND WRITTEN LANGUAGE

1.2   dog 3; moon 3; fish 3; bath 3; rabbit 5; enough 4; study 5; through 3; spaghetti 7; tricky 5.

1.4   Beginning with consonant: 2, 3, 4, 7, 8, 9, 10. Notice that the name of the letter *X* begins with a vowel, even though *X* is a 'consonant' letter. The reverse is true for letter *U*.

1.5   1 CV; 2 CCV; 3 CVCC; 4 CCVCC; 5 VCVC; 6 CVCCCVC (for almost all speakers the initial sound of *you* comes after the *p* – very few speakers say *dispoot*); 7 CCVCVCV; 8 CVCC; 9 CCV; 10 CVCC (8 and 10 are homophones, of course).

1.6   (a) *Rhotic answers*: 1 CVC (or CVVC); 2 CVCVC (or CVVCVC); 3 CVCCVC; 4 CVCVC; 5 CVCVCVC (the final *ng* represents a single nasal sound for most speakers; if a separate *g* is pronounced, the word will be CVCVCVCC); 6 CCCVCVCV (only one C for the double *rr* spelling; instead of the final -CVCV, many speakers will leave out the *e* vowel and just say -*bry*, -CCV); 7 CVCVC (same comment as 6 regarding *rr*); 8 CVCC; 9 CVCVC (*th* represents a single consonant sound); 10 CVCCVC; 11 CVCCVCC (the *t* is likely to be missed out except in an artificially precise version); 12 CVCCVC (*wr* represents just [r] – notice that *write, rite, right, wright* are homophones; no-one pronounces the *t* of *wrestler*).
(b) *Non-rhotic answers*: 1 CV (or CVV); 2 CVCV (or CVVCV) – notice that the *r* which is not pronounced in *near* is pronounced in *nearer* because of the vowel which now follows; 3 CVCV; 4 CVCV; 5 CVCVCVC (or CC at end depending on accent spoken – see comments above); 6 CCCVCVCV or CCCVCCV

(see rhotic 6 above); 7 CVCV; 8 CVC; 9 CVCV; 10 CVCV; 11 CVCCVC (assuming no *t*); 12 CVCCV.

1.7 *Son* and *sun* are homophones in some accents, but not in others; *bill/bill, seen/scene, tick/tic* and (as far as we know) *flee/flea* are homophones for everyone; the two words *tear* are homographs but not homophones. The pairs *eyes/ice* and *fleas/fleece* are distinct, though obviously very similar.

UNIT 2 PHONETIC TRANSCRIPTION, CONSONANT AND VOWEL SOUNDS

2.1 1 kVbVnVt or kVbnVt; 2 tVlVfVn; 3 VmbrVlV (only one [l]); 4 sVptVmbV(r) ([r] in rhotic accents only); 5 gV(V)st (*gh* is pronounced [g] again here – like in the earlier *spaghetti*; both V and VV are acceptable – we haven't yet dealt with this kind of vowel); 6 hVsV(V)VvV(r) – the word does not begin with [w] (*wh* in this word is pronounced [h]; alternatively, you may have an accent that does not have [h] at all, in which case the word begins with a vowel sound, [u]: VsV(V)VvV(r)); 7 sVntVpVd; 8 mVlVnkVlV (if you already know a bit of phonetics, you might have got [ŋk] – that's fine; *ch* is pronounced [k] here); 9 fV(V)tVgrVfVk; 10 bVzwVks (*x* is pronounced [ks] here – two sounds, but only one letter); 11 sVlVfV(V)n; 12 kwVb(V)l – *qu*, with a very few exceptions such as *queue* and *Qom*, is pronounced [kw] at the beginnings of words; the V between [b] and [l] is optional.

2.3 1 [glu]; 2 [kɑm]; 3 [kul] (except for speakers who pronounce the final l-sound as a vowel, in which case the utterance has a CVV formula and cannot be fully transcribed at this stage); 4 [sifud]; 5 [kɑpɑk] ([kɑrpɑrk] if rhotic); 6 [flu] (the phonetic transcription is identical with the spelling form, but the apostrophe which some people use in writing to show the connection with *influenza* obviously has no place in the transcription); 7 [rubɑb] ([rubɑrb] if rhotic; *rh* is pronounced [r]); 8 [uz]; 9 [swit drimz] (some speakers may replace the t-sound with what we call a glottal stop, [ʔ]; notice that the final sound of *dreams* is a [z]); 10 [pliz].

2.4 1 *key quay*; 2 *two too* (also *to*, though the word can be pronounced differently in running speech); 3 *boos booze*; 4 *cruise crews* (*crews* may be different if you're Welsh); 5 *steal steel*; 6 *seem seam*; 7 *week weak* (*weak* may be different if you're Irish); 8 *blue blew* (these may be different if you're Welsh); 9 *freeze frees frieze*; 10 *heart hart*.

2.5 1 sVŋk; 2 fVŋ (fVŋg if you have the type of Midlands/north-western speech identified in the chapter); 3 kVŋdVm; 4 bVgVnVŋ (or with final [g], see 2); 5 bVŋV(r) (or with [-ŋg-], see 2); 6 plVŋk; 7 VŋkrVsVŋ (Vn is also possible at the beginning; and/or with final [g], see 2); 8 VŋkV(V)V(r)dVnV(V)tVd (again, Vn is possible at the beginning; V(V)V means at least two vowels, and optionally three, the extra one being inserted between the two that everyone can agree about; similarly V(V) means at least one vowel, optionally two); 9 VnnV(V)n (*kn* is pronounced [n], so don't be tricked into expecting [ŋ]; also notice one [n] contributed by *un*, another at the beginning of *known*, so the result is a double-length [nn]. In fairly rapid running speech the double [nn] might get shortened, but if the word is said with a single length [n] slowly and in isolation it would probably strike us as *un-own*, which we'd have to interpret as a coined word meaning something like *disown*); 10 VŋgrV; 11 VŋglVnd (a pronunciation without [g] is also possible); 12 lVŋ(k)s (pronunciations with and without [k] are possible, but the nasal is always velar).

2.6 1 fjumz; 2 hjumVn; 3 kVmjunVkV(V)t; 4 lunV(r) (notice no [j]); 5 mVdjul (or the [dj] may become the same as the first sound of *jazz* giving mVCul); 6 mjuzVk; 7 kVmpjutV(r); 8 VmpjunVtV; 9 spekjVlV(V)t (the sound after the [j] isn't actually [u], but if you wrote spekjulV(V)t you can count it right); 10 spektVkjVlV(r) (see 9 for comment on the vowel following [j]).

2.7 1 green; 2 part; 3 heat; 4 kneel/Neil; 5 plume; 6 been/bean; 7 sleep; 8 tense; 9 room; 10 tart.

2.8 1 Eve eats red meat; 2 Ken needs ten cents; 3 Sue leaves next week; 4 Steve's roof leaks; 5 Neil's guests soon left; 6 Palm trees . . . heat . . . deep blue sea . . . two weeks soon went; 7 Lou's suit's dark blue; 8 New brooms sweep clean; 9 Bread needs yeast; 10 Menu / pea soup / beef stew / red beans / steamed leeks / stewed prunes / cream / tea.

2.9 If you're stuck trying to think of alternative spellings, don't forget double letters – a single [p] sound is spelled with *pp* in *happy*, etc.

We couldn't use *hotel* as the keyword for [h] because even speakers who don't 'drop h's' may pronounce this particular word without [h]. *Whisky* is no good as a keyword for [w] because many speakers (Scots, North American, Irish) pronounce [hw] at the beginning of this and many other words spelled *wh-*.

UNIT 3 CONSONANTS: THE ROLE OF THE LARYNX

3.1 The intervocalic consonant is voiceless in 3, 7 and 12. All the rest are voiced.

3.2 One such list could be:

Voiceless	*Voiced*	
upper	robber	runner
otter	rudder	ringer
ochre	rugger	away
offer	rover	awry
author	other	allow
grocer	razor	beyond
usher	leisure	
ahoy!	ledger	
poacher	rumour	

3.3 Words beginning with voiceless consonants are: 1, 2, 5, 6 and 7. All the rest are voiced.

3.4 Words ending in voiceless consonants are: 2, 3, 5, 7, 8, 10, 12 and 14 (and 11, depending on your accent – a speaker of Scottish English might well say [buθ] while one of Southern British English would say [buːð], the colon showing that the vowel lasts a bit longer as well). The rest are voiced (and 13 and 15 don't end in a consonant sound at all!).

You should also note that some speakers have what we call a spelling-pronunciation for 10 which ends with a voiced sound.

3.5

[s]	[z]	
ceiling	zoo	laser
rice	ooze	isn't
ritz	was	rise
use (n.)	husband	use (vb)
	easy	advise (vb)
	blazer	

3.6 (a)

1. [nets]	2. [ʃaks]	3. [rifs]	4. [staz]
5. [slivz]	6. [triz]	7. [kjubz]	8. [legz]
9. [lips]	10. [ʃuz]	11. [tʃamz]	12. [sinz]

(b) The pattern discernible here (and which should be borne out by your additional data) is that we add [s] when a word ends in the singular with a voiceless consonant and [z] when it ends with any voiced sound. (This, of course, excludes what happens when the words ends with [s z ʃ ʒ tʃ dʒ] in the singular.)

3.7 Every English word contains at least one voiced segment because, almost invariably, it contains a vowel.

3.8 1. [p t k]
2. [b d g l m n]
3. [p b t d k g]
4. Voiceless consonants always seem to occur at the beginning of the word, in initial position.

3.9 Two things are being highlighted here: regional accents and the general trend among younger speakers to enhance their regional accent rather than suppress or change it (as was often the case with older speakers who grew up at a time when regional accents were frowned on).

The regional pronunciation would be [juːf] while the 'standard' or 'codified' norm is [juːθ]. Both final consonants are voiceless sounds and both are a bit scraping or hissing (the technical term 'fricative' is discussed in detail later); the regional one is made using the lower lip and the upper front teeth and the standard one using the tip of the tongue at the upper front teeth.

3.10 Almost certainly, the pronunciations intended are ones where the t-sound is not pronounced (and which we can eventually transcribe fully as ['gæʔwɪk] and ['fʊʔbɔl]). The gap is intended to suggest the brief interval of silence which replaces the t-sound that would be used by speakers with other accents (the silence being the auditory effect of [ʔ], the glottal stop).

UNIT 4   MORE ABOUT VOWELS

4.1 Closer vowels in each word pair are: 1 food; 2 book; 3 green; 4 six; 5 feet; 6 scheme; 7 her; 8 see; 9 felt; 10 mist.

4.2 The words are: 1 moon; 2 court/caught; 3 heap; 4 glass; 5 could; 6 crumb; 7 shove; 8 people; 9 word (also *whirred* for most speakers); 10 heart/hart. Rounded vowels are found in 1, 2 and 5.

4.3 In SBE, the lip positions would be: 1, 3, 6, 8, 10 unrounded, rounded; 2, 5, 7, 9 rounded, unrounded; 4 both rounded.

4.4   Schwa is likely to be found in all the syllables in bold print:

At the gate **of the** town **the** con**queror** paused **and** stopped **to** drink **from a** bottle **of** wine **that a** sol**dier** pro**duced from a** bag. **At a** sign **from** the Em**peror the** troops ad**vanced and** en**tered the** town. **Applause** greet**ed them for** the con**queror was popular. The** ty**rant** ru**ler of** for**mer** days **was** brought **to** the exe**cutioner from the** prison cells. **But the** con**queror was** gene**rous and** spared **the** man's life – **a** ges**ture that** led **to** mur**murs of** disap**proval from** the assembled crowd **as** they re**mem**ber**ed the** tor**tures** they **had** suf**fered**.

4.5   This vowel would occur in *murmurs* in SBE.

4.6   1 exercises; 2 agreement; 3 childishness; 4 disadvantage; 5 fortissimo; 6 intoxication; 7 luxurious; 8 recluse; 9 equivalence; 10 requirement.

4.7   *Exercise 4.1*: 1 both back; 2 front, back; 3 front, central/back; 4 both front; 5 back, front; 6 central, front; 7 central, central/back; 8, 9, 10 both front.

Exercise 4.3: 1, 3, 6, 10 front, back; 2, 7, 9 back, front; 4 both back; 5 back, central; 8 central, back.

4.8   They relate to [uː] and [iː] respectively. [w] is made with the back of the tongue and rounded lips (like [uː]) and [j] is made with the front of the tongue and unrounded lips (like [iː]).

   In common with sounds such as [p], [b], [ʃ], etc., [w] and [j] can be the first sound in a syllable and have a vowel following straight after: *pear, bear, share* and also *wear, yeah*! Also like these other *bona fide* consonants, they can never occur in the vowel-slot in the middle of syllables. Finally, if we want to say *a wasp, a yacht*, for example, we use [ə] ('a') just like *a pear, a share*, etc.; we don't use [ən] ('an') as we would for words beginning with a vowel (*an apple, an egg*, etc.).

4.9   We have written [ʷ] beneath the segments with rounding in our realisation of this phrase – yours may, of course, be different.

['w eə   w   ə   'j   uː ə 'jɪəɪ ə'gə   ʊ]
  ᵂ   ᵂ   ᵂ   ᵂ   ᵂ   ᵂ

UNIT 5 THE ORGANS OF SPEECH AND PLACE OF ARTICULATION

5.4 1 apex of tongue; 2 back of tongue; 3 front of tongue; 4 lower lip; 5 back of tongue; 6 apex or blade of tongue; 7 lower lip and front of tongue; 8 lower lip.

5.5 1 hard palate; 2 upper lip or upper front teeth; 3 upper front teeth or (rear of) alveolar ridge or hard palate; 4 upper lip or upper front teeth and velum or uvula; 5 alveolar ridge and hard palate; 6 alveolar ridge.

5.6 (a) 1, 10 lower lip and upper lip; 2, 14 apex of tongue and teeth; 3, 4 lower lip and upper front teeth; 5, 7 back of tongue and velum; 6 front of tongue and hard palate; 8, 9, 11, 15, 18 apex of tongue and alveolar ridge; 12, 13, 16 apex or blade of tongue and alveolar ridge; 17 apex of tongue and rear of alveolar ridge.

   (b) 1, 10 bilabial; 2, 14 dental; 3, 4 labiodental; 5, 7 velar; 6 palatal; 8, 9, 11, 15, 18 alveolar; 12, 13, 16 alveolar; 17 postalveolar.

5.7

Place of articulation	Voiceless sounds	Voiced sounds
Bilabial	p	b m
Labiodental	f	v
Dental	θ	ð
Alveolar	t s	d z n l
Postalveolar		ɹ
Palatoalveolar	ʃ tʃ	ʒ dʒ
Palatal		j
Velar	k	g ŋ
Glottal	h	
Labial–velar		w

5.8 1 boy, match, banana, etc.; 2 tea, see, centre, etc.; 3 wet, winter, wonderful, etc.; 4 view, very, vicious, etc.; 5 shoe, champagne, chip, etc.; 6 you/yew, yellow, yes, etc.; 7 pay, plosive, pink, etc.; 8 care, queue, king, etc.; 9 think, three, thoughtful, etc.; 10 red, riot, royal, etc.

5.9 1 time, sob, robe, etc.; 2 hiss, hate, sort, etc.; 3 sing, bag, rogue, etc.; 4 have, give, save, etc.; 5 itch, wish, cloche, etc.; 6 fill, fun, fade, fuzz, etc. (there are four different voiced alveolar sounds in English); 7 top, hope, soap, etc.; 8 rack, cheque, bake, etc.; 9 oath, bath, giveth, etc.; 10 cough, waif, stiff, etc.

5.10 1 labiodental; 2 velar; 3 bilabial; 4 alveolar; 5 (inter)dental; 6 palatoalveolar.

5.11

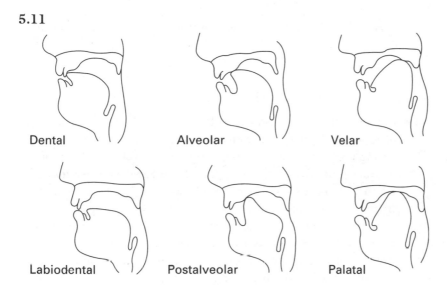

Dental Alveolar Velar

Labiodental Postalveolar Palatal

5.12 1. [ˈtɹaɪ tə bi ˈveɹi ˈkwɪk]: [t] (×2) voiceless alveolar; [ɹ] (×2) voiced postalveolar; [b] voiced bilabial; [v] voiced labiodental; [k] (×2) voiceless velar; [w] voiced labial–velar.

2. [ɪts ˈfeəli ˈiːzi, ˈwʌns ju nəʊ ˈhaʊ]. [t], [s] (×2) voiceless alveolar; [f] voiceless labiodental; [l], [z], [n] voiced alveolar; [w] voiced labial–velar; [j] voiced palatal; [h] voiceless glottal.

3. [ˈdʒʌdʒ ðə ˈvɔɪsɪŋ ˈfɜːst]: [dʒ] (×2) voiced palatoalveolar; [ð] voiced dental; [v] voiced labiodental; [s] (×2), [t] voiceless alveolar; [f] voiceless labiodental.

4. [ˈnɪəli ˈfɪnɪʃt]: [n], [l] voiced alveolar; [f] voiceless labiodental; [ʃ] voiceless palatoalveolar; [t] voiceless alveolar.

5. [ˈtʃek ði ˈɑːnsəz ˈkeəfli]: [tʃ] voiceless palatoalveolar; [k] (×2) voiceless velar; [ð] voiced dental; [n], [z], [l] voiced alveolar; [s] voiceless alveolar; [f] voiceless labiodental.

The transcriptions here make use of [i]. This vowel is commonly used in SBE in unstressed position at the very end of a word. For example, it is the last sound in the word *happy* [ˈhæpi] (and for this reason, it is known as 'the happy-vowel'). It is very like [iː] in quality, but never as long; in duration, it is more like [ɪ]. If you have selected either of these other two vowels to use at the end of *very, fairly, easy,* etc., that is OK for our present purposes. Speakers with other accents will probably have a different vowel in these positions anyway – speakers with a Northern accent, for example, will have a vowel more like [ɪ] or even [e] at the end of these words, etc.

5.13 (a)

Place of articulation	Voiceless sounds	Voiced sounds
Bilabial	p	b m
Alveolar	t	d n l
Velar	k	g

5.14 Most varieties of English use at least eleven places of articulation. SBE, along with the majority of other accents, does not have voicing contrast at postalveolar, palatal, labial–velar or glottal places of articulation. At postalveolar, palatal and labial–velar we find only voiced consonants, [ɹ] [j] and [w], and at glottal only voiceless, [h] (and [ʔ] for those speakers who use a glottal stop). (Regional exceptions would include speakers of Scottish English who make a difference between words like *wear* and *where*, for example, with voiced labial–velar [w] at the beginning of *wear* and voiceless labial–velar [ʍ] at the beginning of *where*.)

UNIT 6 MANNER OF ARTICULATION AND AIRSTREAM MECHANISMS

6.1 Holding your nose while saying 'nanny' may remind you of the English word 'daddy'.

Yes, English has one other nasal consonant: [ŋ].

6.2

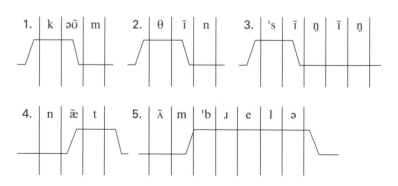

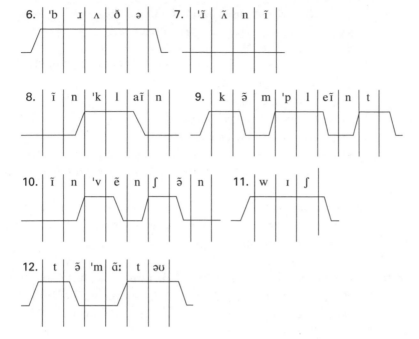

6.3 (The following suggestions are all true only for non-rhotic, non ɟ-pronouncing speakers.)

1. could be *tomb, soon, wrong*, etc.
2. could be *me, now, knee*, etc.
3 could be *comma, funny, singer*, etc.
4. could be *summit, hornet, singers*, etc.
5. could be *amber, answer, anger*, etc.
6. could be *oh!, A, I / eye / aye*, etc.
7. could be *embers, indeed, anchored*, etc.
8. could be *mat, nut*, etc.
9. could be *I'm, in*, etc.

6.4 [m]   as in *mummy*   voiced bilabial nasal
[n]   as in *nanny*   voiced alveolar nasal
[ŋ]   as in *singing*   voiced velar nasal

6.5 The speaker cannot pronounce nasal consonants. This happens when we have a bad cold sometimes.
To indicate the same difficulty, the title was spelled 'Belagcholly days' (*Belagcholly days*, anon., from *A Choice of Comic and Curious Verse*, edited by J. M. Cohen) – you could equally well have written 'Belagcholy', of course.

6.7 1. [m] *time, comb, some, hymn, him, am,* etc.
       [n] *tin, cane, sign, vein, van, done,* etc.
       [ŋ] *sing, rang, hung, ping-pong, wrong,* etc.
    2. [ŋ] cannot occur at the beginning of words in English.
       [m] *moon, might, may,* etc.
       [n] *know, new, gnash,* etc.
    3. [m] *hammer, coma, demand,* etc.
       [n] *honour, Anna, enough,* etc.
       [ŋ] *banger, singer, stringy,* etc. (*g*-pronouncing speakers
            will have a [g] in these words following the ŋ-sound)

6.8 The name Ngaio begins with a voiced velar nasal, [ŋ], in Maori.
     English speakers pronounce this name as [ˈnaɪəʊ] or occasionally
     even with a sort of 'spelling pronunciation' [nəˈgaɪəʊ]).

6.9 1. [naʊ, ənd, əˈgen, dɪstrɪˈbjuːʃən, tɜːnz, kwiːnz, ðen, ˈsevən,
        nəʊ, ˈmænə, ˈhevən, ˈdʌzənt, ðən, wʌns, ɪn, ˈkɒntrækt]
        There are nineteen voiced alveolar nasals altogether.
     2. [kɪŋz]
     3. You will find nasalized vowels in: [nãʊ̃ ə̃nd əˈgẽn ə̃],
        [dɪstɹɪˈbjuːʃə̃n tɜːnz], [juː ˈmãɪt], [ˈkɪ̃z ˈkwĩːnz ə̃nd], [ðẽn],
        [ˈsevə̃n ˈnə̃ʊ ˈtɹʌ̃mps], [ˈmæ̃nə̃ fɹə̃m ˈhevə̃n dʌzə̃nt], [mə̃ː ðə̃n
        ˈwʌ̃ns ĩn ə̃ ˈlaɪftaɪ̃m ə̃nd], [mə̃ʊst], [ˈkɒ̃ntɹækt], [geĩm ə̃v]

6.10 (For [n], the voiced alveolar nasal, see Fig. 6.2 on p. 47.)

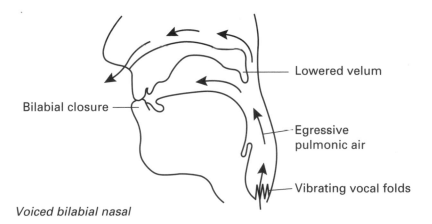

Voiced bilabial nasal

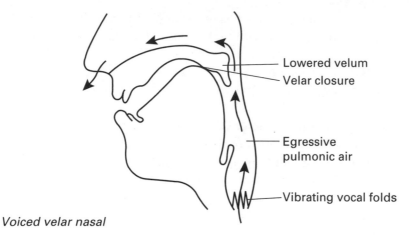

- Lowered velum
- Velar closure
- Egressive pulmonic air
- Vibrating vocal folds

Voiced velar nasal

UNIT 7 CONSONANT DESCRIPTION AND VPM LABELS

7.1 English plosives:

[p]	as in *poppy*	Voiceless bilabial plosive
[b]	as in *Bobby*	Voiced bilabial plosive
[t]	as in *tatty*	Voiceless alveolar plosive
[d]	as in *daddy*	Voiced alveolar plosive
[k]	as in *cocoa*	Voiceless velar plosive
[g]	as in *go-go*	Voiced velar plosive
[ʔ]	as in, e.g. *ar'* (art) or *li'l* (little) for some speakers	Voiceless glottal plosive

7.2 1. sink; crab; stack; loch (when pronounced [lɒk], as a homophone with *lock*, but when pronounced [lɒx] with a more Gaelic pronunciation, this word ends with a fricative); end; gnat; lump; log.

2. pick; glue; chemist; ptarmigan ['tɑːmɪgən]; dump; tree; bread.

7.3

[f]	as in *fluffy*	Voiceless labiodental fricative
[v]	as in *vivid*	Voiced labiodental fricative
[θ]	as in *thirtieth*	Voiceless dental fricative
[ð]	as in *thither*	Voiced dental fricative
[s]	as in *saucy*	Voiceless alveolar fricative
[z]	as in *zoos*	Voiced alveolar fricative
[ʃ]	as in *sheepish*	Voiceless palatoalveolar fricative
[ʒ]	as in *leisure*	Voiced palatoalveolar fricative

The above all form voiceless/voiced pairs. The odd one is:

[h]	as in *ha-ha*	Voiceless glottal fricative

7.4 1. space; phase; scratch (but see also affricates); this; hush; faith.
   2. cosy; raisin; mother; either; cousin; buzzing; easy.

7.5 [tʃ] as in *church* Voiceless palatoalveolar affricate
   [dʒ] as in *judge* Voiced palatoalveolar affricate

7.6 fudge; winch (although this word can also be pronounced [wɪnʃ] ending in a fricative); picture; words (where the final [dz] constitutes a close-knit homorganic sequence of stop + friction agreeing in voice); cats (the explanation for *words* also covers the [ts] at the end of *cats*); cheque; mints ([ts] again); lethargy; joke; watches; refrigerator.

7.8 [w] as in *one-way* Voiced labial–velar approximant
   [j] as in *yo-yo* Voiced palatal approximant
   [ɹ] as in *ring-road* Voiced postalveolar approximant
   [l] as in *lilac* Voiced alveolar lateral approximant

7.10 1. (a) **Plosives** *Bilabials* – [p] in: people, ex**p**ect, po**pp**ing, drip, popular; [b] in: bins, alphabet, nibbled. *Alveolars* – [t] in: turned, last, stalls, no**t**iced, that (x3), different, rest, its, neatly, lettered, it (x3), twenty, letters (x2), alphabet, taste (x2), letter (x2), quite, sweet, just, expect, laughed, two, into, letting, aren't, take, instance, -dusty; [d] in: turned, down, seemed, different, side, lettered, said, do, and (x3), inside, filled, Z (x2), words, informed, good (x2), nibbled, discovered, delicious, you'd (x2), drip, down, confided, dry, -dusty. *Velars* – [k] in: six, like (x2), make, carefully, discovered, quite, ex**p**ect [ɪk'spekt], confided, take; [g] in: good (x2), wagon.

   1. (b) **Fricatives** *Labiodentals* – [f] in: different, from (x2), -self, filled , al**ph**abet, for, informed, carefully, lau**gh**ed, confided; [v] in: of (x3), very (x2), discovered, voice. *Dentals* – [θ] in: mouth; [ð] in: they('re), the (x8), that (x3), with, these, their, them. *Alveolars* – [s] in: last, stalls, noticed, seemed, rest, its, side, small, said, -self, inside, -six [sɪks], taste (x2), discovered, sweet, just, expect [ɪk'speckt], juice, most, so, voice, instance, sawdusty; [z] in: as, stalls, was (x2), bins, letters, Z (x2), these, words, Gs, A's. *Palatoalveolars* – [ʃ] in: delicious; there are no words containing [ʒ]. *Glottal* – [h] in: who, (h)im, here, (h)is (x2), (h)e.

Note that speakers with a London accent may well use [f] and [v] instead of the dental fricatives [θ] and [ð]; Irish speakers may well use the corresponding dental plosives instead of the two dental fricatives.

Note also that whether or not you pronounce all or none of these h-sounds will depend entirely on your accent – the ones in parentheses are ones that might be omitted by all speakers.

1. (c) **Affricates** *Palatoalveolars* – [tʃ] in: **ch**arge, **ch**in; [dʒ] in: char**ge**, **j**ust, **G**s, **j**uice.

2. **Approximants** *Labial velar* [w] in: **w**agon, **w**as (x2), **w**ere, t**w**enty, **w**ith, **w**ords, quite [kwaɪt], s**w**eet, **o**ne [wʌn]. *Palatal* [j] in: **y**our-, **y**ou'd (x2), knew [njuː], popular ['pɒpjələ]. *Alveolar lateral* [l] in: **l**ast, **l**ane, sta**ll**s, Mi**l**o (x2), neat**l**y, **l**ettered, -se**lf**, fi**ll**ed, a**ll** (x2), **l**etters (x2), a**l**phabet, peop**l**e, **l**ike (x2), nibb**l**ed, carefu**ll**y, **l**etter (x2), de**l**icious, **l**aughed, **l**etting, popu**l**ar, **l**ow.

UNIT 8 THE INTERNATIONAL PHONETIC ALPHABET

8.1 palatal 1, 7; uvular 2, 3, 10; bilabial 4; alveolar 5, 6, 8; velar 9.

8.2 1. nasal 1, 3; plosive 2; fricative 4, 6, 10; implosive 5; lateral approximant 7; tap 8; approximant 9.
2. voiceless uvular affricate 2, 10 [q͡χ]; voiceless bilabial affricate 4 [p͡ɸ]; voiced alveolar affricate 6 [d͡z].
3. Lateral fricative.

8.3 close vowels [i y u]; close rounded vowels [y u]; back unrounded vowels [ɑ ɑ̃]; nasalized vowels [ɛ̃ œ̃ ɑ̃ ɔ̃] front rounded nasalized vowels [œ̃].

8.4 1 [θ]; 2 [n̥]; 3 [ɓ]; 4 [lʲ]; 5 [k̚]; 6 [βz]; 7 [uː]; 8 [a]; 9 [ỹ]; 10 [ɔ].

8.5 1 voiced retroflex nasal; 2 voiced uvular plosive; 3 voiceless velar fricative; 4 voiceless alveolar lateral fricative; 5 voiced postalveolar approximant; 6 voiced velar implosive; 7 voiced labiodental approximant; 8 voiceless alveolar lateral click; 9 voiceless alveolar ejective fricative; 10 voiceless palatal fricative.

8.7 1 possible, e.g. [ʟ]; 2 impossible because a closed glottis is required to initiate the egressive glottalic airstream and therefore simultaneous vibration for voicing is not possible; 3 possible, [çʷ]; 4 impossible because a closure in the pharynx (if this was possible) would block the airstream before it could reach the nasal cavity; 5 possible, [ỹː]; 6 impossible because the tongue tip cannot articulate at the alveolar ridge and the palate at the same time; 7 possible, [ɰ̃]; 8 impossible because the highest part of the tongue cannot be simultaneously at two different heights (close and open-mid); 9 possible, [ë]; 10 impossible, the bilabial aperture cannot be simultaneously narrow enough for friction and wide enough for a (frictionless) approximant.

UNIT 9 MORE ABOUT CONSONANT VARIATION

9.1 *Obstruents*

Voiceless		*Voiced*	
[p]	bilabial plosive	[b]	bilabial plosive
[t]	alveolar plosive	[d]	alveolar plosive
[k]	velar plosive	[g]	velar plosive
[f]	labiodental fricative	[v]	labiodental fricative
[θ]	dental fricative	[ð]	dental fricative
[s]	alveolar fricative	[z]	alveolar fricative
[ʃ]	palatoalveolar fricative	[ʒ]	palatoalveolar fricative
[tʃ]	palatoalveolar affricate	[dʒ]	palatoalveolar affricate

Sonorants – all voiced

[m] bilabial nasal, [n] alveolar nasal, [ŋ] velar nasal; [w] labial–velar median approximant, [j] palatal median approximant, [ɹ] postalveolar median approximant, [l] alveolar lateral approximant.

With the exception of [h], the obstruents all participate in voiceless/voiced pairs.

9.2 Your lists will include:

Voiceless

[p] in keep, spirits, up, appetite, produced, chops, repast, past, unprepared, helping, happy, champagne

[t] in that, at, invitation, great, into, flat, spirits, appetite, midnight, produced, it, repast, time, Tony, finished, must, strength, past, telephone, Mr (mister), it's, what's, Charlotte's, right, to, comfortable, let, daughter, what, wanted, don't, sitting, bottle, midst, toasts.

Your list for [t] may depend on your accent and/or on how aware you are of how other people speak and pronounce things. For some speakers, [t] will only occur at the beginning of words or syllables; [t] at the end of a syllable will be replaced with [ʔ] If you have a popular London accent, for example, your [t] list may include items like *invitation, into, appetite* (note only the first letter t is pronounced [t] in this word), *time, Tony,* etc., but you will have put words like *that, at, great, flat* and *spirits* into a separate list where the letter t triggers the pronunciation [ʔ]. This is not a problem.

[k] in   keep, cabbage, (for some speakers) strength, woken, Queen, OK, check, comfortable, thank, woke, drank, conventional

[f] in   friend, flat, for, finished, half, finally, telephone, comfortable

[θ] in   strength, thank

[s] in   spirits, greasy, chops, served, repast, must, strength, said, past, voice, Mr (mister), it's, Charlotte's, say, Mrs (missus), what's, sitting, midst, toasts

[ʃ] in   invitation, should, she's, finished, Charlotte's, champagne, conventional

[tʃ] in   gargantuan (or [-tj]), chops, which, check, much

Voiced

[b] in   cabbage, been, by, Newby, born, comfortable, baby, bed, bottle

[d] in   idea, should, and, midnight, would, friend, moved, produced, served, mounds, unprepared, said, daughter, wanted, don't, mind, bed, drank, midst

[g] in   great, gargantuan, greasy

[v] in   evening, invitation, of, moved, have, voice, very, conventional

[ð] in   that, the, with

[z] in   was, mounds, as, his, is, Mrs (missus), Newby's, she's, means

[ʒ] in   –

[dʒ] in cabbage

The suffixes agree in voicing with the sound at the end of the stem: *spirit* ends in voiceless [t] and *spirits* ends in voiceless [ts], *Newby* ends in voiced [i] and *Newby's* ends in voiced [iz]; *produce* ends in voiceless [s] and *produced* ends in voiceless [st], *move* ends in voiced [v] and *moved* ends in voiced [vd]. The only departure from this is where the stem ends in a related sound, in which case we need to add a vowel to the realization of the derived form, for example, *cabbage* ending [dʒ] would yield [ˈkæbɪdʒɪz], *want* ending [t] yields [ˈwɒntɪd].

[θ] is less frequent and is found in words like the noun *strength* and at the beginning of *thank,* while [ð] is very common, occurring in the frequently used grammatical words like *this, that, the,* etc.

9.3

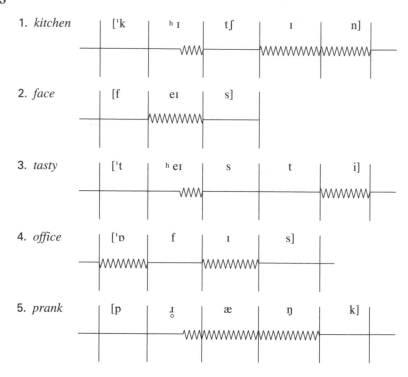

1. *kitchen*

['k   ʰɪ   tʃ   ɪ   n]

2. *face*

[f   eɪ   s]

3. *tasty*

['t   ʰeɪ   s   t   i]

4. *office*

['ɒ   f   ɪ   s]

5. *prank*

[p   ɹ̥   æ   ŋ   k]

9.6

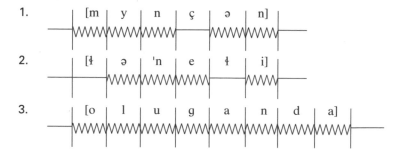

1.   [m   y   n   ç   ə   n]

2.   [ɫ   ə   ˈn   e   ɫ   i]

3.   [o   l   u   g   a   n   d   a]

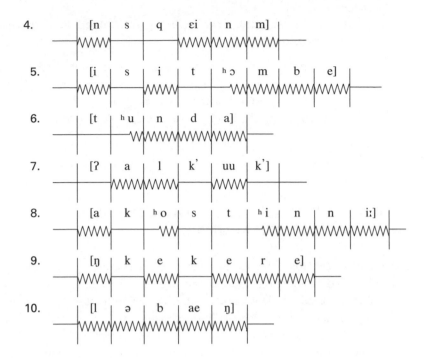

4. [n s q ɛi n m]

5. [i s i t ʰɔ m b e]

6. [t ʰu n d a]

7. [ʔ a l k' uu k']

8. [a k ʰo s t ʰi n n iː]

9. [ŋ k e k e r e]

10. [l ə b ae ŋ]

9.8 Your lists will include:

Aspirated

[pʰ] in pretty, pencilled, pink, paws.

[tʰ] in fairy-tale, tail, tabby (x2), tip, tiny, to.

[kʰ] in kitten (x2), cat, cream (x2), cream-coloured, carpet, climbed, crept.

Note that in words like *kitten, enchanting, delicate, subtle, pretty, smoky, outlined, sitting, exotically, beautiful, carpet, worshippers, inspecting* where the [p, t, k] are not initial in a stressed syllable and words like *it, delicate, cat, shape, back, front, stomach, black, neck, dark, pink, tip, straight, beast, sat, carpet, not, at, stalked, that, crept, sheet*, where they come at the end, there may be rather less aspiration and so they have not been included in this list.

Unaspirated (in *s*-clusters)

[p] in inspecting.

[t] in stomach, streaks, straight, stalked.

Other examples of unaspirated [p t k] included those followed by another consonant sound in final position: *six* ([sɪks]), *weeks, streaks, cheeks, stalked, crept*.

Possible glottal reinforcement

[p] in shape, tip.

[t] in   it, delicate, cat, straight, beast, sat, carpet, not, at, that, crept, sheet.

Note that many speakers today will go one step further and completely replace the final t-sounds in these words with [ʔ]: [ɪʔ wəz], ['delɪkəʔ 'feəri-], ['kæʔ huːz], etc.

[k] in   back, stomach, black, neck, dark, pink, stalked.

Also:

[tʃ] in   inch

UNIT 10 YET MORE ABOUT CONSONANTS: SECONDARY ARTICULATIONS

10.1 1 voiceless labial–alveolar plosive; 2 voiceless labial–palatal fricative; 3 voiced labiodental–alveolar fricative; 4 voiced labial–uvular plosive; 5 voiced labial–alveolar nasal; 6 voiced alveolar–velar plosive; 7 voiced labiodental–palatal approximant; 8 voiced labiodental–postalveolar/labiodental–palatoalveolar fricative; 9 voiced alveolar–uvular trill; 10 voiced labial–velar fricative. *Note that regardless of which order the symbols occur in, we have systematically given the most forward place of articulation first in the label – compare 3 and 10, for example.*

10.2 double: 1, 2, 5, 6, 7; single or sequential: 3, 4, 8, 9, 10.

10.3 Because they involve two simultaneous complete closures in the oral cavity, a velar closure and one more advanced (bilabial, dental, alveolar, etc.).

10.4 Because they involve two simultaneous strictures of open approximation, one at the lips and a lingual one somewhere between palatal and velar.

10.5 Your list will include: absolutely [lʷ]; stretch [tʷ]; morning [mʷ]; silhouetted [sɪlʷu'etɪd]; frosted [fʷ]; door [dʷ]; few [fʷjʷ]; from [fʷ]; hand would (said slowly) [hændʷ wʊd] (otherwise [hænd əd]); frozen [fʷ]; halfway [fʷ]; nose or [nəʊzʷ ɔː]; incredibly [kʷ]; truth [tʷ]; etc.

10.6 [t]   voiceless alveolar plosive
[k]   voiceless velar plosive
[kʷ]   labialized voiceless velar plosive
[b]   voiced bilabial plosive

[bʷ]   labialized voiced bilabial plosive
[m]   voiced bilabial nasal
[mː]   long voiced bilabial nasal
[mʷ]   labialized voiced bilabial nasal
[mːʷ]   long labialized voiced bilabial nasal
[n]   voiced alveolar nasal
[ŋ]   voiced velar nasal
[ŋː]   long voiced velar nasal
[r]   voiced alveolar trill

10.7 Your lists will include:

Palatalized – flapping, Is**le** of, briskly, planned, long, pilot, lonely (x2), reversa**l of**, **all a**, baffling, Learning, sailors, like, Monthly, club, Let, ha**l**yards, live, daily, English, perfectly, simplest, sailing, cleat, lift; *Velarized* – hauled, Gosfield, shamble, sails, roles, world, trouble, single, salty, sprinkle, unable, help; *Devoiced* – planned, cleat, club.

The letters given in bold in the palatalized list here indicate positions where you might expect a dark-l (because the l-sound is at the end of a word) but where, because a vowel follows, the l-sound is in fact clear-l. So, you would get *all* [ɔːɫ] with a dark-l, but *all a* [ɔːlʲ ə] with a clear-l. The same thing happens in the word *halyards* – we also use clear-l before the [j] in the standard kind of southern British accent used here.

INDEX